The Future of Service is

5D

why humans serve best in the digital era

Jaquie Scammell

'Jaquie Scammell's *The Future of Service is 5D* **powerfully presents an innovative and transformative approach** that integrates physical, cognitive, emotional, social, and spiritual components into an optimal, human-centered service model. **This book is essential for anyone looking to blend technology and human service harmoniously.** What are you waiting for? Buy this book NOW – your customers will thank you.'

Joseph Michelli, Ph.D. Professor of Service Excellence and *New York Times* #1 bestselling author of *The Starbucks Experience, The Zappos Experience, Driven to Delight,* and *Prescription for Excellence*

'A mindful pause for any leader navigating the service industry. **I loved it; humanistic, realistic, practical, actionable.**'

Lorie Argus
Chief Executive Officer
Melbourne Airport

'Jaquie Scammell's *The Future of Service is 5D* **is a profound exploration of the evolving nature of service in the digital age.** Drawing from her extensive experience and insightful observations, Jaquie delves into the critical need for a human-centered approach in customer service, especially in an era dominated by technological advancements. Her concept of 5D Service – encompassing physical, cognitive, emotional, social, and spiritual dimensions – provides a comprehensive framework for understanding and excelling in service roles today. **This book is not just a call to action for improving customer service; it's a clarion call** for reinvigorating humanity's role in an increasingly automated world. Through compelling narratives and practical insights, Jaquie champions the indispensable value of human connection in service, making **this book a must-read for leaders, service professionals, and anyone interested in the future of customer relations.**'

Peter Cook
Author, entrepreneur, Ishaya monk

First published in 2024 by Jaquie Scammell

A catalogue entry for this book is available from the National Library of Australia.

ISBN: 978-1-923007-4-51

Printed in Australia by Pegasus
Book production and text design by Publish Central
Cover design by Stacey Jospeh

The paper this book is printed on is certified as environmentally friendly.

CONTENTS

ABOUT THE AUTHOR

Jaquie Scammell is an award-winning author of *Service Habits* 2nd ed. and *Service Mindset*. She is an eminent keynote speaker, a thought-leader in the field of service and is the CEO and founder of ServiceQ – a business which partners with other organisations to reimagine their service culture by developing conscious service leaders, engaged employees and loyal customers.

Jaquie has enjoyed a diverse career with over 25 years of leadership experience in public, private and not-for-profit sectors starting with the McDonald's franchise system and expanding to major sports and entertainment venues such as Wembley National Stadium (UK), Emirates Stadium (UK) and the Australian Open Grand Slam. Her industry experience has helped her adapt concepts to a range of contexts.

She is a relational skills expert who is acutely focused on practices to be more present in our day-to-day interactions and ensure our humanity is felt in all culture and service conversations and actions. Her passion is to develop service leaders and ignite transformative customer service behaviours that stick. Jaquie believes we are in a new era of taking care of people, and first we need to understand how to take care of ourselves and our teams, so that we can better serve others.

INTRODUCTION

Imagine you're on hold for some assistance. Your only lifeline is a robotic voice stating, 'Your call is important to us, please hold'. You finally connect, only to realise you're speaking to a perfectly balanced and precise AI-generated voice, reciting the menu options in a monotone, mechanical voice. It doesn't ask you how your day was; it's devoid of empathy. We've all been there, frustrated and shouting at an automated system.

Now, you're standing in a physical queue, greeted by Sarah, a human employee. She seems distracted, and her interactions are robotic in their predictability. She rattles off a script of instructions, never truly engaging with you. Despite being served by a human, you feel just as isolated as you did listening to the robotic voice on the phone.

The two experiences may leave you pondering: 'When did human service become almost indistinguishable from being served by a machine?' We've never been more connected, yet human service feels more distant than ever.

Imagine a world where you engage with service professionals who aren't just doing their job but serving with intention and awareness. Envision a digital platform where convenience doesn't come at the cost of human connection but enhances it. This isn't a utopian dream; it's a vision we can manifest together. We can make it a reality by integrating 5 dimensions – physical, cognitive, emotional, social and spiritual – into a human-service approach. This is 5D Service.

Welcome to *The Future of Service is 5D: Why humans serve best in the digital era*, a book that aspires to redefine our understanding of what service means in an increasingly digital and interconnected world. The journey from frustration to fulfilment starts here.

My journey to 5D Service started 3 decades ago when I first entered the world of customer service. Over those decades, the human element has kept me going – the smiles, the relief on people's faces, the genuine 'thank yous' that no automated system can replicate. However, I've noticed a chasm growing between techno-logical capabilities and human essence in service in the encroaching digital era.

This book was born from years of research, practical experience and a burning desire to bridge that gap. My work has been inspired by many teachers, including Professor Robert Sapolsky, Deepak Chopra and Yuval Noah Harari, along with the seven dimensions for defining what makes us human: mental, physical, social, financial, spiritual, environmental and vocational.

If you've picked up this book, it's likely that you, too, sense the seismic shifts happening in our society. Whether you're leading a team, business or community, and whatever the area – government, education, medicine, food production, technology, media, entertain-ment – you'll have noticed that the phrase 'customer service' doesn't evoke the enthusiasm it once did.

Service industries are madly rushing to digitalise for efficiency, compromising what once set them apart – the act of service by a human. It's a crucial juncture in time, and digital technology isn't just an accessory but an integral part of our lives, altering how we communicate, work and even think.

As we move swiftly into an era of artificial intelligence, robotics and automation, it's easy to succumb to the narrative that machines will replace humans in almost every field, including service. And it's even easier to miss the nuances that make human service irreplaceable. For any leader in service, the new dilemma is how to reclaim the human in 'human service'.

This book offers a mindful pause to reconsider the path we're heading down. What if I told you that, far from making humans obsolete, the digital era will bring a more dynamic, authentic form of service than we've ever seen before?

5D Service is a new paradigm that brings the quintessential human qualities of service back into the limelight.

This book will equip you with a new framework for understanding and implementing service – a 5D approach that leverages the strengths of both humans and technology. You'll learn what these dimensions entail, how to harmonise them, and how to lead a revolution in your own sphere of influence.

So, are you ready to transform your frustrations into a vision for a more humane, more fulfilling future? Are you prepared to participate in a revolution that places the human spirit back at the heart of service? The Future of Service is 5D. The future is now.

HELPFUL BELIEFS FOR READING THIS BOOK

Before you dive into this book, please know we will have a much larger conversation about service than you may think. Following are some helpful beliefs that will set the stage and enable the book to help you create change. You may disagree after reading these beliefs and decide to put the book down. I won't take offence. However, if you resonate with these beliefs, you'll gain incredible value from this book.

Helpful belief #1: Everyone is a customer and a human

You, me and everyone moving throughout the world need goods or services in some shape or form – everyone is a customer.

There's a stigma around the word 'customer'. When I say 'customer care', it immediately narrows people's thoughts to a tiny sliver of a business or a small group of people who work in call centres, behind counters and on shop floors. Shift to this mindset and we will shift our behaviours towards each other. We are all in service to one another.

Helpful belief #2: You can change the world, one customer at a time

How many times are you a customer in a typical day or week? How many times do you interact with staff working for a brand or business who help you solve a problem or give you an answer?

It's time to deprogram what we think customer service is and begin to view it as an extraordinary function in our world. When we do this, we'll serve and lead in a way that influences humanity through small, daily service interactions.

The future of service is about creating a ripple effect that reaches beyond the individual customer to impact society at large. Sometimes, we don't tackle the big issues in life because they feel, well, big. This book (like all my books) is full of pragmatic suggestions, recommendations and tools to make this 'big' idea accessible.

Part 1

HOW WE GOT HERE

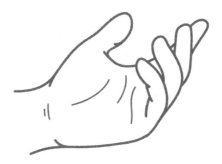

1. CUSTOMER SERVICE DIED IN 2020

We are in a bit of a mess. We're at a pivotal point in humanity's history where we could be overwhelmed with sadness and devastation if we take stock of what we have become as a species.

- **Our natural world is under threat**. I'm no expert in climate change, and I find the conversations on this matter extremely complicated. Yet, as I move throughout the natural world each day, I see how consumerism, capitalism, greed for profit and economic growth are disastrously affecting our environment.
- **Our society's social justice issues and the fact that our democracy is under threat have locked people into fear**. Most weekends, when I walk past the steps of Parliament House in downtown Melbourne, Australia, I'm met with banners and protesters screaming their pleas for truth, justice and fairness.
- **Our youth are affected by a mental-health crisis like nothing ever seen before**. According to the American Centers for Disease Control and Prevention (CDC), nearly three in five teenage girls (57 per cent) said they felt 'persistently sad or hopeless' in 2021. That was the highest rate in a decade. And 30 per cent said they had seriously considered suicide – a 60 per cent increase over the previous 10 years (CDC, 2023).

I feel like I've only scratched the surface of the big issues we face today, and as if these weren't enough to create a sense of despair and a crisis of trust, along came the COVID-19 pandemic!

Regardless of where you were in the world and your story around 2020, you would most likely describe that year as characterised by confusion, disorder or even failure.

The changes that took place across society have manifested in various ways, and the mess and chaos of 2020 led to heightened emotional vulnerability and stress among customers and employees – and anyone, really, with a heartbeat. I'm not surprised. We were operating in survival mode.

When you chunk down from the world macro issues into your patch of the workplace or corner of society – the day-to-day inter-actions and comings and goings of family life, work life and being a community member – it was all being redefined before our eyes.

The great reset. New order. New world. New normal. These phrases were being bantered around like new slang in a kids' play-ground, and our idea of what 'good' looked like was thrown up for debate. It was almost like we were being permitted to reorganise and redefine what comes next. However, during this period, one of the casualties was the quality of human-to-human service interactions.

As a leader in the workplace, this time was incredibly poignant. Staff and customers were pushing boundaries in ways that made leaders look in the mirror and question everything.

RIP customer service

Customer service, as we knew it before the pandemic, is dead. Gone forever. This is a new era, a new incarnation. And it's having a shaky, Frankenstein-like start to life.

Maybe it's unfair to blame the pandemic for the death of customer service. Perhaps we were already on a slippery slope; perhaps 2020 just shone a spotlight on the lack of deeper purpose in people's lives or on customer service staff's inability to apply service skills when under significant pressure.

Slowly, the resilience of communities, workplaces and individuals weakened, taking the spirit of service with it. If there were already cracks appearing in the workplace culture between colleagues, these were exposed. If a customer's loyalty was already questionable, it didn't survive. If a relationship wasn't built on a solid foundation, it was tested beyond breaking point. And my oh my, were some of our most intimate relationships tested! We all had to dig deep to deal with our individual situations.

We were challenged to look at what was perhaps always there, but there was now nowhere to hide. Everyone's world got smaller. Borders closed, schools closed, global travel came to a halt, and people were forced to stay at home within their local bubble. They could see, maybe for the first time, any disconnect, any absence of purpose in their life – or simply what they were escaping each day when they left home.

Altered expectations

Cast your mind back over the pandemic period.

I recall trying to rent a car. The employee who eventually answered the phone said, 'Yeah, nobody answers the phone these days . . . Oh, and we don't have any cars to rent'.

I recall my first overnight stay in a hotel in one of the moments of freedom outside the multiple lockdowns. Housekeeping? No chance. Room service? Not happening.

I recall the restaurant experiences where the wait time for food was over an hour, yet the restaurant was half empty.

I recall the 7-month delivery time for a new couch. That was just the new norm.

I recall going to a luxury day spa for a massage for the first time in 2 years and being presented with a disposable cup filled with beautiful tea, which used to be served in delicate glassware to match the environment . . . and the price.

Yes, I acknowledge these were unprecedented times. But whether it was due to staffing shortages, supply-chain issues or businesses that decided to leverage the situation to lower the expectations of customers and, therefore, lower their costs, the result was that service took a massive hit.

It's part of human evolution for societal norms and values to change, influencing the standards we expect from the world. But the changes from a pandemic are often accelerated and forced – at least, that's what it felt like to me, having lived through this one.

So, it's no surprise that people's expectations of themselves, others and the brands and businesses they interact with have altered in the wake of COVID-19. The question is, 'Has service been resurrected, or have we lowered our expectations forever?'

Service died because there were no staff

My team and I worked with some incredible companies during the peak of this crisis. I recall often speaking with leaders in major stadiums, airports and other venues who were short thousands of the employees needed to serve the crowds of customers coming through their doors.

In June 2022, in Australia (and most of the Western world), almost a third of employing businesses (31 per cent) had difficulty finding suitable staff (Australian Bureau of Statistics [ABS], 2022). For many frontline staff who stayed – scared, under-resourced and perhaps being given unrealistic expectations to deliver on – the volume of their voice was louder, and employees had more say in their work conditions.

During the pandemic, some organisations prioritised caring for and supporting their people; others did not. The organisations that quickly identified that 'healthy staff equalled healthy customer service' emerged strong. The company leaders realised that the staff they did have coming to work were under stress and, given their lack of motivation and weakened resilience, needed extra support and care. The organisations that turned their attention to their workforce resurrected customer service quicker.

They were helped, at first, by an undertone of, 'Customers will forgive you if you can't measure up to what they were used to before the world went bonkers'. But towards the end of 2022, the message and tone changed. I vividly remember saying to leaders, 'Customers will be less forgiving in 2023. It's now assumed and expected that you've returned your staffing levels to where they were and that you've reorganised your operations to deliver excellent service again'.

The world of work is evolving

When people change how they work, it changes how they serve.

In mid-2022, a pilot of a 4-day work week commenced across 90 companies in the UK and Australia, organised by not-for-profit 4 Day Week Global (4dayweek.com). These companies committed to implementing the 4-day-week model without reducing staff wages, with the promise from staff that they would commit to 100 per cent productivity at work. Who would have thought, hey? Back in 1980, Dolly Parton sang:

'9 to 5
Yeah, they got you where they want you
There's a better life
And you think about it, don't you?'

Well, here we are in 2023, and we're no longer just thinking about it; we're making changes, Dolly!

Workplaces have been propelled into remote work and virtual meetings. Work is in the home more than ever, and home is at work. We're Zooming with people at their kitchen tables, meeting their children and pets, and judging their virtual backgrounds or artwork on their walls.

Workplace flexibility has dramatically changed and now encompasses work-life balance, physical and emotional health and family care. Work that isn't restricted to trading hours and premises can be done anywhere, at any time, format, or structure.

For leaders, it's tricky to set the direction of employees when the world of work is evolving at the speed of light and even trickier when the customers' behaviours are also evolving. Perhaps the more flexible the workplace becomes, the more flexible the resurrection of service has to be, with far greater adaptability required in how service is delivered.

Customers' behaviours are evolving

Customers' behaviour is also changing in response to post-pandemic life, and it's still not clear if the dog is wagging the tail or the other way round. One way of thinking about it is that customers' behaviours are changing due to us all becoming accustomed to a poor level of service, and therefore not demanding anything unique or extraordinary anymore.

Here's an example. Once upon a time, a big purchasing decision like buying a car or renovating a home seemed straightforward. Now, the demand for materials and manufacturing has slowed the customer journey down, creating a whole new layer of touchpoints and disappointment, and lowering customer expectations of speed and convenience. Supply-chain disruptions since COVID-19 have led to product shortages and delays. According to the ABS, more than two in five businesses (41 per cent) faced supply-chain disruptions in June 2022, down from a peak of 47 per cent in January 2022 (ABS, 2022).

Another way of thinking about changing customer behaviours is that customers are demanding safer and more convenient ways of doing business with a brand and demanding service from the comfort of their homes.

The pandemic forced businesses to adapt their operations and customer service frameworks. Telehealth consultations became mainstream during the pandemic, mainly out of necessity. However, post-pandemic, it was clear that consumers had become more willing to use telehealth than before COVID-19 and that providers were more willing to adjust their work practices.

In the same way, Uber Eats led the way during lockdowns, offering contactless orders and delivery. There's no need to exchange menus, cash, credit cards or even a smile – and this hasn't changed post-pandemic.

Or have customers' behaviours changed because people's motivation and resilience were tested beyond belief during the pandemic? And because there's been a subtle ripple effect from the reduced social interaction due to social distancing, remote work, lockdowns, travel restrictions and so on? Let's not forget just how extreme this was at the time. In my wonderful state of Victoria, Australia, you were limited to moving within a 5 km radius of your home and barred from leaving home after 8 p.m. I never thought I would see such a time in history.

Logic would say that these shifts and changes in working and being served by each other meant that people had fewer opportunities to interact with others and, therefore, got out of practice with their social skills. It appears that this, in turn, altered our expectations of customer service; it felt like people were extremely forgiving at first if they were on the receiving end of a miserable human interaction from an employee, knowing that the employee was not coping and was just trying to get by in an out-of-control world.

However, this patience appears to have worn off over time, and we've ended up with fluctuating customer tolerance levels. Businesses are trying to clamber their way back to pre-COVID-19 ways of working and serving people and wondering why they can't achieve that.

Fluctuating tolerance levels

'They lost it at me.' 'They blew up in front of two other staff.' 'They went off at me.' These are phrases that a group of retail professionals used in a live webinar with one of our facilitators to describe how a colleague behaved towards them. I was shocked.

If you're not familiar with these bits of slang (I'm in Australia, don't forget, and we have a somewhat strange way of talking at times), what those phrases mean in plain English is that the person yelled at them quite explosively.

This is not okay. None of us would condone this behaviour, yet it's happening increasingly from both customers and staff. Sadly, you only have to google 'abuse of service staff' to get a flood of surveys, studies and new reports from different industries and countries. It's sort of accepted information at this stage that it's 'normal' for service staff to cop abuse.

As society changes, people's tolerance for different behaviours, attitudes and beliefs can also shift. Some people have dialled up their resilience to various things in the past few years and can bounce back quickly. Their tolerance may have decreased in other areas, though – they might be impatient with slow responses or intolerant of misinformation, for example. We will examine this grumpy, sensitive behaviour more deeply in Chapter 3.

Our motivation was under attack

To give service, you need a healthy dose of motivation. However, motivation isn't permanent; it's temporary and needs renewing each day, especially when you're serving fellow humans with all sorts of needs and emotions to navigate. You need to feel motivated to smile; you need to feel motivated to listen actively; you need to feel motivated to problem-solve and go above and beyond to find a solution to something that may not be obvious. You need to feel motivated to let the other person, in some cases, save face, even when they're in the wrong.

But being motivated by something external, such as money or entertainment, won't cut it when we're constantly surrounded by loss, stress and fear. Eventually, the spirit in each of us wants something more purposeful. Superficial motivation leads to superficial behaviour, and under pressure, it ultimately leads to unstable emotions because we can no longer keep faking the 'expected behaviour'. We're exhausted; we've had enough.

Our resilience was under attack

From 2020 to a good part of 2022, many of us were swimming in a cesspool of tragedy and bad news. People lost their lives, their loved ones, their businesses, their jobs and their freedom. People lost control. And this meant that there was more division and less unity among people.

Something as simple as behaving kindly and compassionately towards another human being is difficult when you cannot manage your own emotions. No matter how skilled and well-trained you are in service or how strong your soft skills are, if you cannot self-regulate, you cannot access those skills when you need to.

Onwards

The past has happened, and we can't change it, but we can change what happens next.

The pandemic has shifted us into a time when it feels like no one can hold others to account for anything anymore, and many people just want someone to blame and to fix the mess we find ourselves in.

But what if focusing on the future of service in your patch of the office, your neck of the woods, your corner of the world, is a way through this mess? What if we're all playing a little too small? We're looking for someone to blame for what we've become as a global collective, feeling that it's such a behemoth job to address the issues that we become paralysed, leading to inaction. What if we were to play a bigger game, to serve each other much better than we have been of late?

To serve means to put the needs of others first and work to benefit others in some way. As a concept, service can be critical in creating a more sustainable and equitable world where people's needs are met across multiple dimensions.

- **When we serve our natural world**, we promote sustainability by reducing waste and pollution and engaging in practices that protect our natural resources. We remember where we came from and, with respect, serve the plants, animals and planet to keep healing us and giving us back life.
- **When we serve society, we promote social justice.** Service can help address social inequalities and promote greater equity by helping marginalised communities and, without judgement, advocating for social justice and human rights.
- **When we serve the health of others**, we improve health outcomes in our community by promoting healthy living practices and providing access to medical care in poor pockets of our communities.

Whatever your role – whether you're a CEO, head of a team or department or perhaps an emerging leader – looking for direction and setting direction is critical for the future. It starts with small, ordinary actions of daily service. Over time, they will change the direction of humanity.

By working together and engaging in acts of service, each of us in our workplace, communities and homes can positively impact the world. Now, I'm no unicorn, nor am I a powerful politician. I am a person, just like you, who can create a legacy not based on what I do personally but on what I help others do.

The current state of play on this planet propels me into action day and night – I want to do my bit through a lens of service. Service is necessary. Service is essential for our future. Let's look at where we're heading and how this may impact how we lead and serve our people, customers and society. Let's prepare, think a little differently and perhaps let go of some of our legacy ways of thinking and make room for the new.

The future will not be like the past. Strap in, and I'll get my crystal ball.

2. THE FUTURE ≠ THE PAST

'Life is not about waiting for the storm to pass.
It's about learning to dance in the rain.'
—Vivian Greene

Each day, as I become more aware of the rapid changes happening in society, the number of directions this chapter could take multiplies. The saying 'What got you here won't get you there' has never been truer.

With every death, there is a birth, and we are birthing something new. It's a wonderful time to be alive and be a leader who serves and influences how others serve. New ways of thinking will be required to lead organisations and lead a new way of serving customers. To influence the future of service, I'm suggesting we start by narrowing in on the role of technology and the role of humans to understand the sweet spot between them.

At this point, it's probably relevant to share that I was born in the late 1970s. This means I'm in awe of and fascinated by where digital technology has taken us; it also means I have to work a little bit harder to stay up to date because advanced technology isn't something I was born into. It isn't intuitive for me. For example, I was the remote control for my family's TV. If someone wanted to change the channel, I had to get up and turn the dial myself.

I turned on my first computer in a computer class at 15. In my teens, I didn't have a mobile phone: I spoke to my mates at night on a phone attached to the wall in the living room. If you were lucky enough to have a second phone in the home, another family member might 'accidentally' pick up halfway through your conversation. When we finally got the internet in our house – this amazing thing promising to change our lives – we couldn't speak on the home phone while the internet was being used.

Cash was king and credit cards were processed with a heavy, sliding metal contraption and a bunch of coloured carbon copy papers; it was far easier to write a cheque than it was to use a credit card. The term 'kiosk' meant a building at the beach where we would go and buy ice creams and bags of candy with our loose change.

The drive-through at McDonald's was a novelty and the quickest way to get fast food. Whenever you walked into a store or up to a counter, you were served by a human. The closest we got to self-service was the salad and dessert bar at Pizza Hut: an absolute novelty.

Now, life without digital technology almost seems unimaginable. Children as young as 12 months old use iPads and computers for education and entertainment. A landline phone in the home is rare. Everyone has a device that is always with them, not just for communication but for information at their fingertips, location-finding and safety reasons. Today, we get Wi-Fi on planes. I'm using it right now to write this book!

Nowadays, we see signs saying, 'We are a cashless store', and people use credit cards via their phones (thank goodness, because I've often left the house without my actual credit cards!).

Nowadays, thanks to the many home delivery services, you can order food through an app and have it on your front doorstep within minutes.

Nowadays, a 'kiosk' replaces a customer-facing staff member, allowing companies to save on labour costs and customers to self-serve, check-in, checkout and get on with their day without ever speaking to a human.

Our world moves fast. It is designed to help us get what we want when we want it. Our world is slowly removing humans from service interactions at every possible turn. Robots are taking over our world. Is that a little too dramatic? Okay, perhaps a more accurate way to say it is that many tasks these days are being done by technology coded to perform that task.

Technology is destroying and evolving service at the same time

If we take a balanced view, this digital revolution is not being driven entirely by big tech companies – you and I are also driving it, thanks to the sneaky and profiteering focus of big tech companies on persuading us how to think, how to behave and who to identify ourselves as.

Remember when social media first hit your mobile device? Think back to the 2000s. Slowly, subtly and stealthily, we were persuaded – some may say manipulated – to change our behaviours. The novelty of being 'liked', 'loved' and 'followed' provided a steady release of dopamine that made us feel good. Remember when the function of 'tagging' people in photos was introduced?

A thumbs-up or love-heart emoji on a photo of someone you knew was a social, tribal way of showing others that you acknowledged them.

Remember, too, when the messaging apps started making three moving dots appear while someone was responding to you? It was designed to keep you on the channel and online until you got the response. Our unconscious need for a response, validation or the continuation of a conversation meant that we stayed online and connected to our devices for longer.

Many reputable software engineers, investors, founders and computer scientists who worked to create the algorithms at Google, Facebook, Instagram, YouTube and Pinterest have said in some way that social media is not a tool for making our lives easier or better – it's manipulation, using your own psychology against you. I've never heard a parent say they want their kids to spend more time on social media. Have you?

Just as social media has changed how humans behave, other technology is changing how we serve people across all service interactions. We need to wake up to this now, to look into the crystal ball and see what potential threats are coming our way instead of being swept up in the magic of technology.

Technology is reconditioning the way we interact and cope with the human stuff. It's mostly unconscious, fed by our need for and addiction to productivity, speed, convenience and greater efficiencies in the workplace and life.

The internet has made it possible for us to shop and access information at any time of day and night. As a result, we now expect businesses to be available 24/7 to answer questions and provide support. Companies that fail to offer round-the-clock support risk losing us to competitors who do.

The savvier we become with technology, the faster we expect response times. We expect increasingly quick and convenient ways of getting products and services, and demand efficiencies in doing business with brands. The high bar set by companies like Amazon, with their same-day or next-day delivery options, has normalised quick delivery times. We expect personalisation, self-service options and instant gratification. The way things used to be in service, before many technological innovations kicked in, is almost unimaginable now; perhaps we wouldn't choose to return to the way things used to be.

The digital revolution has caused a significant shift in how we live, work and communicate, and continues to impact our daily lives profoundly.

To understand the future of service, we need to understand the future of AI

AI tech has been around for many decades: the term 'artificial intelligence' was coined at the Dartmouth Conference in 1956, often considered the birth of AI. During this period, researchers built the first AI programs, which could play games like checkers and solve algebra and logic problems.

Some interesting AI statistics as of 2023, according to the Techjury article '101 Artificial Intelligence Statistics' by Josh Wardini:

- AI can increase business productivity by 40 per cent.
- The number of AI startups grew 14 times over the previous 20 years.
- Investment in AI startups grew 6 times since the year 2000.
- Some form of AI is present in 77 per cent of our current devices.
- By the time I finish writing this book in 2023, there will be 8 billion AI-powered voice assistants.
- Some 72 per cent of business executives believe that AI will be the most significant business advantage in the future (Wardini, 2023).

I'm no AI expert, but I'm fascinated by these statistics and how AI is changing how we work. AI has already made us more efficient in the workplace. For example, robotic automation of Amazon's warehouse operations, introduced in 2012, reduced their order processing time from 90 minutes to under 15 minutes. Did you know an estimated 10 per cent of nursing activities by humans could be replaced by automation by 2030? The Techjury article is worth a look, and it's only the tip of the iceberg.

Chatbots have also taken a seat at the workplace table, and the more sophisticated they become, the more opportunities we have to enhance the customer experience. It's estimated that 85 per cent of customers' relationships with business enterprises will be managed without human involvement. AI gives customers more real-time communication faster.

I take a deep breath in putting this next stat down on the page: according to the World Economic Forum's (WEF) report, The Future of Jobs 2020, automation may displace 85 million jobs by 2025. However, the report also estimated that 97 million new jobs would be created – new roles that generate, manage and maintain the automation technology, as well as roles to manage the ethics, safety and security associated with it (WEF, 2020).

In all revolutions, certain jobs go away, and new jobs are created:

- Lamplighters used to go around and light the gas streetlamps at dusk, but once we brought in electric streetlamps, that job was unnecessary.
- Switchboard operators are no longer needed, with manual telephone switchboards mostly phased out.
- Bank tellers were replaced by Automated Teller Machines (ATMs).
- Checkout staff are slowly being replaced by self-checkout technology and online purchasing.
- Video store employees have disappeared entirely with the rise of streaming platforms.

In addition, jobs have been created that didn't exist in the 1800s, opening up opportunities for people – professional service roles such as computer programmer, data scientist, web designer, aerospace engineer, renewable energy engineer, video game designer and social media manager.

But is this AI revolution the one that will reduce the largest number of jobs?

AI will definitely enhance many jobs – make them easier, more fun and higher paid – and create new jobs that we can't foresee yet. Excellent. This is good news, right? It makes sense that technological advances will give us time back and make our lives easier. I've heard it said that it once took 85 per cent of the population to work to feed everyone in a village, and now it only takes 2 per cent. So, if we're not doing the tasks needed to feed the village, what exactly are we all doing? From where I see things, working across various countries and immersed in multiple companies, we seem to be still working, and working pretty hard at that, even given the post-pandemic changes to work! What will we do in the future, and what will our purpose be in the day-to-day workplace?

According to McKinsey's report 'Jobs lost, jobs gained: Workforce transitions in a time of automation', automation could replace 30 per cent of the human workforce globally by 2030 (McKinsey & Company, 2017). So, if we hand the role of front-facing service over to intelligent robots, what will the role of humans be?

Front-facing customer service roles are at risk of extinction

I believe front-facing service roles are at risk of extinction. Why?

<ChatGPT has entered the chat.>

ChatGPT is the fastest-growing app in human history, and generative AI is changing humans and how we serve each other. It hugely reduces our need to think critically and creatively, problem-solve, and apply emotional reasoning to our responses and written replies.

Instead of just being ordinary chatbots, ChatGPT, Google Bard, Microsoft Bing and so on, use generative AI. This means that each day, they're learning more ways to generate their own new answers from the data that we, the public, are searching and prompting for.

In episode 367 of the Lex Fridman Podcast (25 March 2023), Sam Altman, the CEO of the company behind ChatGPT, OpenAI, said that the category of jobs that will be impacted the most by ChatGPT is customer service. He believes there'll be way fewer jobs relatively soon, particularly in call centres and frontline services, because ChatGPT and GPT-4 language models will become better at these jobs than human beings – and 10 times more productive.

Of course, Altman and other leaders in the AI development space are well aware of the technology's potential negative consequences. In 2023, Altman and the CEOs of Google, Amazon, Meta, Anthropic, Inflection and Microsoft made voluntary commitments to self-regulate their AI offerings. According to Stanford University's 2022 AI Index, some 37 AI-related bills were passed into law globally in 2022 in attempts to regulate and reduce the risks of AI (Artificial Intelligence Index, 2023). The European Union passed its comprehensive Artificial Intelligence Act into law in June 2023.

Putting aside the deeper issues with AI and the world's attempts to deal with them, let's ask a simple question: What will be the quality of service if we allow AI to do it all for us?

I've heard it said that AI is already as good as the **average** doctor at providing diagnoses, as good as the **average** lawyer at weighing up probability and risk, and it's as good as any **average** worker at knowledge work such as information synthesising and processing. It's even as good as the **average** management consultant in a business setting. But who wants **average**?

Perhaps generative AI will become better than average the more it learns and retains knowledge. Still, knowledge is never enough to create extraordinary service interactions. Knowledge is gathered from learning, while most would say that wisdom is gathered from day-to-day experiences and that we reach a state of 'being wise'.

Wisdom is the sophisticated 'science' needed in service – experience through the lens of humanity, from the heart, combined with the practical ability to make consistently good decisions in service interactions.

Our creativity, innovation and genius come from being wise. It's the application of knowledge and the discernment that comes from perspective. In service interactions, a robot or machine may have the ability to know what to say, but a human being (the greatest technology) will have the wisdom to know when and how to say it.

Who wants average? The service pyramid

There are times when we want to be served by technology: we want the efficiency.

There are times when we want to be served by humans: we want the connection.

There are times when we want both.

Enter the service pyramid.

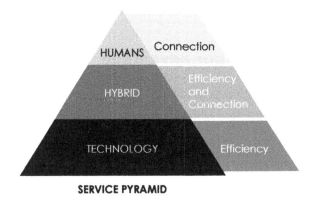

SERVICE PYRAMID

'Too many modern companies have replaced
a person with a number and mistakenly called
that number a customer.'

(Sinek 2022)

Humans are at the top of the pyramid – we do the connection parts of service best. We need to remember that at the heart of service is humanity. We have names, hearts and minds; we are spiritual beings having a human experience and thrive from connecting with other humans. AI and digital solutions often provide an average experience focused on an outcome: to get the job done. But getting the job done doesn't mean it's done exceptionally well. Average service doesn't impress us. Who wants to be average?

If you're genuinely interested in being extraordinary in service, not average, and in bringing service excellence, then technology is just an enabler. You are still the composer and conductor; technology alone won't raise the bar for the future of service. In the digital era, humans serve best when they know when to leverage their human qualities and when to let technology do its thing.

Being human is our advantage

Being human is a privilege and a purpose in itself.

While technology is grabbing everyone's attention, we forget that service roles always require a level of presence and attentiveness. The unwritten task for every person in service is to make each person they serve feel like they're the only person in the room.

Can you recall what it feels like to be served by someone who is present – someone who makes you feel in that moment that you are important and gives you their undivided attention?

Our minds think tens of thousands of thoughts a day – we're addicted to thinking and already have to work hard to stay attentive before the distractions of notifications and devices. Now, modern technology is competing for our attention, too. But giving attention in service interactions – one-to-one, one-to-many, leaders to employees or employees to customers – is the advantage that humans have over robots. It's why humans will always serve best, if we know how to hold our attention and give our attention.

Good judgement and uniquely human skills make a difference in people's lives: AI and robots (at least for the moment) can't give attention or offer connections the way humans can. It might be able to turn its view to see from a different angle, but it cannot give attention. It's the skill of paying attention (rather than just following or giving instructions) that is our advantage. It's critically important to polish, refine and shape this skill for the future of service.

Here's an example of how crucial human attention, judgement and connection can be. In October 2022, I was involved in a car accident in Nice. My partner and I had been travelling for 28 hours from Australia and were keen to get to our accommodation to rest our heads. Our car was hit from behind by a tanker truck carrying LP gas; we were pushed several hundred metres down a five-lane motorway and eventually smashed into a concrete barrier. The car was a write-off, but we were both unharmed – a miracle.

The service agent at the rental car office, Mathieu, had no idea we'd be involved in such a serious accident 15 minutes after he sent us on our way. But it was his humanity that I believe saved our lives.

You see, our booking in the system was for a small car. It would have been easy for Mathieu to process the booking as it was and keep moving through the very long queue behind us. But something told him to slow down, ask questions and determine our needs and wants on this European driving holiday. His curiosity, his awareness of his own senses – paying attention to our needs – led him to upgrade us from a Fiat Punto to a larger SUV – and of course, the larger car had all the safety features and more metal to protect us at the time of impact.

This story is just one example of millions of ordinary interactions employees have with customers daily, impacting their lives in extraordinary ways.

In the future, the digital revolution will enable sophisticated robots to give you instructions for:

- taking your medicine,
- applying for a home loan,
- buying a car, and even,
- giving you advice and support for grief and loss.

These are examples of robots serving humans during meaningful experiences. These are the moments in life that matter – experiences that most of us would remember and suggest are significant. They require compassion and attention, and yet, for speed and convenience, we may well turn them over to machines.

As with anything in life, it's about balance. We need to get really good at being human so that, at the very least, whatever is fed into the machines is as close to a caring human as possible. If we don't go into this era of humanity with our eyes wide open, before we realise it, AI will have completely taken over and be impacting the entire system, like a cancer that has slowly spread. We need to diagnose early and start treatment to maintain a strong level of humanity in the workplace, both through creating the most ethically sound AIs possible – because let's face it, AI is here to stay – and, most importantly, redefining the need for humans in customer-facing job roles.

Technology is advancing exponentially, but human physiology – our brains – has not evolved at all. And yet, we are magnificent and magical. We have abilities within our multilayered dimensions that it's time to utilise and expand fully –tech cannot replace that.

I would suggest a future in which humans work with robots but are not controlled by robots is a great harmonious vision to hold on to. Because if we're not careful, we'll start believing that robots are better than us. And that is simply not true.

Leaders, your job now is to look at the touchpoints of service in your business that require technology and the touchpoints that need humanness. The sweet spot for the future is the hybrid of technology and the 5 dimensions of service in your teams, workplace and business. This is how we rebirth service, allow our collective magic on this planet to be seen and keep humans at the top of the service pyramid rather than letting technology rule our world.

3. WHY 5D SERVICE IS NECESSARY FOR THE DIGITAL ERA

If humanity is our service advantage, then now, more than ever, we need to tap into the 5 dimensions – the 5D – and embrace a more human approach to service. Hell, what have we got to lose? Customer service died in 2020, remember?

The old saying, 'Happy staff equals happy customers', remains true in theory. The only *massive* difference is that keeping people happy – staff or customers – is a bloody tough gig these days.

We cannot keep pulling out the same tricks. To think that the past indicators of employee and customer happiness will equal the future indicators of happiness is a bias in our thinking. Everyone who leads teams, businesses, political parties and industries must realise that we will disappear in the new era unless we evolve our leadership approach to service and how we serve our people and customers. It might sound a tad dramatic, but hear me out.

Customers are grumpier, and staff are ultrasensitive, which means leaders need to get really good at the human stuff, or they'll be left behind. For example, are you afraid to speak your mind in case you upset or offend someone else? Are you reluctant to ask others to stay back, work harder or put in some extra effort in case you are blamed for bullying? Sometimes, everything appears 'acceptable', and no one is held accountable for poor behaviour.

Is it getting harder to work together – newer and older generations – because our short-term thinking and individualistic approaches mean we're not very good at setting aside our immediate wants and desires for the long-term good? The absence of a collective vision as the human race is slowly eroding how society works.

There are more significant issues in society, but these are happening right in front of us. The way the lady serves us at the drycleaners. The way the telecom provider speaks to us on the phone. The way the elderly gentleman wipes the table down in a café. The way the young recruit scans groceries at the store.

The ordinary moments between an employee and a customer are, at scale and speed, conditioning society's norms and what's considered acceptable. In this way, customer service is critical to the future of our humanity.

WTF? Since when do we have to remind people to be kind?

I was standing in a queue at the security screening point of a busy airport last week, watching the digital screens above with their key messages reminding all customers to be kind. I then listened to the flight crew's announcement over the PA system, again, reminding us to be kind to fellow passengers and crew. Last week, I walked into a café and was greeted by a sticker on the counter asking me, as a customer, to be kind. These messages left me feeling that we're fighting to sustain kindness in our society – and this is perhaps more serious than we think.

I recall, during the tumultuous years of the pandemic, the sudden influx of notices appearing on shop windows, the tops of counters and in communal lobby areas saying things like:

'Our staff are doing their best. We thank you for your patience. Shouting, swearing, insulting or abusive behaviour will not be tolerated under any circumstances. Anyone considered to be abusive will be asked to leave.'

Of course, this was due to the social behaviours that followed the trail of devastation for all sized businesses serving the general public, who were continually letting people down and delivering substandard service as they navigated the uncharted waters of the pandemic. As discussed in Chapter 1, crippling staff shortages and supply-chain problems were just some of the major issues leading to the dropping of customer service standards.

The resulting display of tantrums from customers was breathtaking. At the extreme end, here in Australia, Sydney real estate agent Ellen Bathgate was punched in the face by an angry ex-tenant, resulting in her first ever black eye. Then there was the Perth nail salon customer who had cuts, bruises, chipped teeth and a concussion after an alleged assault by a fellow customer. Not what you'd expect from a routine property inspection or a regular manicure!

Some industries and workplaces had to deal with more violence and abusive customers than others. For example, according to a *Herald Sun* article, in 2022, more than 9000 healthcare workers were abused, threatened or assaulted across Melbourne's major hospitals (Booth, 2022).

The wave of notices that appeared was deemed necessary for staff psychological safety and wellbeing, and judging by my recent experiences, things haven't improved.

What a world we're in that we need to teach basic common manners and courtesy. And yet, here we are. Many people are still in self-preservation and self-protection mode, having dealt with so much fear and trauma during the pandemic – and kindness was one of the first traits to be impacted.

There used to be an unwritten law that kindness and compassion were the basis for how you approached others and operated in the world. According to biologists such as Darwin, cooperation has been more important to our success in humanity's evolution than competition. For the human race as a species, compassion has been critical to our survival and ability to thrive. So perhaps it's the kindest of us who will survive these crazy times and the years ahead with the least pain and resistance.

Can kindness be learned and relearned? Is it inherent or changeable? I want to believe that we are fundamentally kind, even if maybe that kindness gets lost sometimes. So where do we, as a society, need to focus on dialling up our kindness so that the whole human race can evolve?

Well, look no further than the person who next serves you – a fellow human being interacting with you to:

- provide you with a product or service
- fix your problem
- help you
- care for you.

If they have an attitude of kindness, they can access empathy and tap into your needs more effectively.

Right now, people in customer-facing roles are critical to kindness surviving and to keeping our society alive and thriving. Small acts of kindness can go a long way these days, and they can completely turn situations around to become far more uplifting and positive.

Grumpy customers need 5D Service

The old way of thinking about a grumpy customer or a customer complaint was to view the unhappiest customers as your greatest source of learning. Perhaps this was born from an idea that grumpy customers were an anomaly – a rare moment in a week. A grumpy customer required significant conversation, discussion and reprimand with all staff involved – it was an opportunity to pull the team together and learn what went wrong. What did or didn't we do? How can we make sure this situation never happens again? How can we ensure the grumpy customer forgives us and wants to return and be loyal to our business?

I'm not sure businesses are even listening to grumpy customers these days, let alone learning from them. This could be because we're desensitised to them, given the spike in dissatisfied people and the fact that anyone can review your business negatively at any time. Or it could be because employees are dealing with their own emotional worries. Either way, it seems like a grumpy customer is no longer seen as a gift.

Realistically, if you're a business that serves many customers in a day, you can expect the odd dissatisfied customer from time to time.

In October 2020, Talkdesk Research found, in a global study, that 58 per cent of retail customers said their expectations of customer service were higher than one year previously (Talkdesk, 2021). Higher expectations, sure, but why the aggression? And how is this impacting the way staff show up at work?

I'm unsure what comes first: whether staff aren't coping with grumpy customers or are ultrasensitive to any complaint or discomfort in an interaction. All I know is that we need to break the cycle if we want to rise above dissatisfaction and improve the culture of a business and the workforce's happiness, creating happiness for the customer.

The number-one rule in customer service is to leave the customer better than you found them. So, if grumpy customers are here to stay, frontline staff and leaders in business need to get really good at dealing with customers who aren't happy and have tactics and ways of turning that around. Before we look at how the 5D Service framework will help with this, though, let's first take a closer look at the cycle many employees may be trapped in when it comes to grumpy customers.

A harmful cycle

If a workplace environment is seeing an increase in grumpy, reactive customers, this will feed staff stress. Think of the impact this has on a customer service exchange. When stress is present, it tends to make people more protective of themselves. I'll unpack this further in the section of this chapter about stress. Still, in short, we're seeing more defensiveness and more reactive and thoughtless behaviour.

It's no wonder that alongside short customer fuses, we also see pockets of service with no empathy, service with few to no social skills, and service approaches with little creative thinking or problem-solving and even less flexibility.

One of the companies my business, ServiceQ, has done significant work with over the years is a major airport here in Australia, Melbourne Airport. With over 20,000 employees bringing their emotions and human stuff to work each day in an airport environment, which has been described as a lot like a hospital emergency department, it's fair to say it's a stressful place to work at times. Travellers who move through the airport are on high alert and often need help. One of the key service commitments introduced in their customised service program was 'Be Calm'. All staff in all job roles – cleaners, security, retail, food and beverage attendants – saw the need to build muscle around this behaviour in their workplace. This is not only about helping the worker manage their own stress; it also has a huge influence on how the customer feels. Calm is contagious and critical in heightened environments such as airports.

So, here's where I will say something that's probably not so popular. I'm writing this book to be helpful, not to be liked, so here goes: *Blaming grumpy customers for making customer service harder won't get you far.*

No one should have to face violence at work. However, I do think that people in service roles who aren't trained to deal with the 'human stuff' – the variety of emotions, the unpredictability of customers – will be left behind and will not be able to perform well in a service role, nor will they enjoy their work.

It's another harmful cycle – employees blaming customers for the way they treat the customer – and that cycle will continue unless companies break it.

Take a good look in the mirror as a business and see what you've become. What I'm referring to here is culture. What behaviours do you tolerate that you would like to see less of? What behaviours do you encourage in your staff that you want to see more of? Once these are clearly articulated, give your people permission and a platform to call it out when they see poor behaviour in a service exchange (with both internal and external customers), and provide them with the skills to do this confidently.

Cultivating a strong service culture is not a job for the Head of People and Culture, nor is it the Head of Customer Experience's job – it's everyone's job. Every staff member should be a custodian of the organisation's preferred behaviours and service skills, and this distributed ownership will see sustainable results that stick. When you turn your attention to the relational skills and capabilities of your workforce as a part of the solution, you will influence the DNA of your people.

The bottom line is that we cannot serve customers in a way that leaves them better than when they arrived if we're unable to rise above our stuff – dissatisfaction, fear, stress and anxiety – and put on our professional service uniform and serve.

You can teach all the soft skills and relational skills in the world to help your teams do service better. Still, if they're not coping with their stuff, they won't be able to access those skills, especially on hard days. It's more than teaching people soft skills – it's about helping people self-manage.

Your people need something different

At ServiceQ, we've noticed in the last few years that people are not coping, not just with our airport clients but also those who work in other environments such as stadiums, mining, service departments, call centres, hospitals, aged care, automotive and high-street retail. The thousands of faces we see in training rooms each month across different industries are often people in service roles, dealing with humans each day. An increasing percentage of these people are ultrasensitive.

Even the slightest criticism or negative feedback often deeply affects an ultrasensitive individual. They may overreact to perceived slights or feel overwhelmed by minor stressors. Their sensitivity may lead them to take things personally and interpret actions or words as intentional attacks, even when this is not the case. They might require extra reassurance and support to navigate everyday challenges due to their heightened sensitivity.

In service roles, having a mindset that supports you in times of challenge is useful. For example, not taking things personally is integral to being able to solve problems for customers. This makes sense in 'normal times', but as we've seen, our 'normal' has been challenged somewhat in the past few years. We could blame the pandemic for people becoming ultrasensitive. A study by Headspace.org.au found that 74 per cent of young people reported that their mental health was worse since the outbreak of COVID-19 (Headspace, 2020). We've all experienced some trauma these past few years, and that stuff catches up with you.

We could blame the higher cost of living putting additional stress on people, which has been significant. In June 2023, the Consumer Price Index (CPI) had risen 6 per cent over the preceding year (ABS, 2023).

We could blame social media. Socials are designed to keep us confined and entertained; we feel safe and comfortable inside this bubble. We can relax. No need to worry or think about different ideas or perspectives – the algorithms skilfully feed us whatever confirms our beliefs. Just keep scrolling, liking and commenting. Then, the real world throws a few curve balls, and we wonder why we're so uncomfortable with having difficult conversations and lack resilience.

Maybe the sum of all these things has led us to where we are today. The point is, as much as a percentage of people are still resilient and can deal with what is thrown at them at work and in life, an equal percentage of people are just not coping with the human stuff.

About burnout

In 2022, 50 per cent of Australian employees reported feeling burnt out, according to Employment Hero. In 2023, that number had jumped to 53 per cent (Employment Hero, 2022). While it's only a slight increase, as the report says, it's a trend that should lead employers to consider how they may be contributing to this percentage – increasing or decreasing it.

What is burnout? It's a constant state of exhaustion, making the individual feel unmotivated and unproductive at work. There's more awareness of burnout these days, and employees are seeking greater balance in their work lives than ever before.

Perhaps the sense of being on the edge of burnout contributed to the Great Resignation, where millions of people left their jobs during

COVID. The ripple effect has been immense, with widespread job vacancies and workplaces unable to fill shifts.

Post-pandemic, there has been a change in people's attitudes towards work. Employees question what they do and ask themselves, 'Is it worth it?'

About stress

Stress is a very real threat to your customer service. As a business leader, one of the new indicators that will indeed underpin your customer service performance is how well your staff handle stress.

I used to talk about stress like a small ripple in a calm pond, momentarily disrupting tranquillity. Just as a ripple fades away, so would the minimal amount of stress, leaving little impact.

Today, I see stress having a much longer-lasting and more damaging impact on people. It's not a ripple in a pond but more a raging storm. Its relentless downpour saturates every aspect of life, making finding solid ground or a moment of respite challenging.

Many of your staff are serving customers who are stressed out. They have financial pressures, home life issues and broken families. They may feel disconnected from society. Their mental health may not be great. They may struggle with illness. Your teams need to be able to manage their own stress to serve stressed-out customers and put them at ease with service solutions.

I believe it's critically important to manage your stress response, particularly when dealing with humans as part of your working day.

Seriously. We are all a little stressed out and wound up . . . me included. Staying on top of stress requires constant attention and management practices in the modern-day world because we're under the most considerable amount of stress we have ever experienced in human history (Ray, 2022). Did you know that by 2027, the market revenue of antidepressant drugs across the US is predicted to be more than $25 billion (The Business Research Company, 2023)? Consider how prolonged stress, anxiety, depression and the inability to manage negative emotions modify our human relations.

Today, I just want to help people chill the (bleep) out and give them access to a big toolkit of techniques to help them manage their stress. Okay, I'm off my soapbox now – I guess you can sense I'm passionate about this topic, ha!

The reason staff must manage stress is because it harms your brain and harms your customer service. The science, of course, is that when someone erupts into violence, verbally or physically, it's because the oldest part of their brain – the reptilian brain – has taken over. Stress encourages this part of the brain to take control, and it uses 'fight, flight or freeze' for self-preservation. Stress impairs the brain's pre-frontal cortex, leading to less empathy, antisocial behaviour, reduced creativity and less flexibility.

Humans are not meant to be under constant, high stress; we're not wired for it. Just as we're not wired to sit in front of screens all day, birds aren't wired to see glass windows, and kangaroos aren't wired to expect cars to zoom past when they cross roads. We're not wired to be in a constant state of fight or flight, yet many of us are. Regardless of the hats we wear at any point of the day, no one is immune to the modern-day world, and we all have to function in a more stressful system than ever before.

I've always believed that customer service is not a question of capability or whether people care, but rather of how well people manage themselves under pressure and in different scenarios – how they self-regulate.

Right now, the solution to improved service for businesses is linked to people improving their stress management. Managing the oldest part of the brain and knowing how to bring it back into line is a critical customer service skill for this era.

A new era of taking care of your people so that they'll take care of your customers

Never has the connection between employee wellbeing and customer service been stronger.

One of the questions I've been asking a lot these past few months is, 'How do you change how people work so it transforms the way people serve?' This question is less about procedures and more about what makes people satisfied at work and keen to put their best foot forward, giving the customer in front of them the best version of themselves at that moment.

It's tricky for leaders who have to do more with less, and it's tricky to keep customers happy. If I were to generalise, I would say that customers expect more value for their money, and employees expect more money for less work and effort, so we get a customer service circus. It's like walking on a tightrope. The customers carefully seek maximum value for minimal cost, while the staff balance their desire for higher compensation with the expectation of reduced workload. Both parties must maintain their equilibrium, delicately navigating the thin rope of compromise. Any misstep could lead to a fall into the chasm of dissatisfaction and unmet expectations.

One thing I do know is that employees are loyal to workplaces that care about them. In a 2022 survey by Employment Hero, employees who rated their employer's commitment to wellness as 'good' were more than 63 per cent more likely to say they were loyal to a business (Employment Hero, 2022).

We are all a little bit more entitled now than we were a few years ago, and maybe our definition of being 'taken care of' by an employer has also altered. We are all walking that tightrope, seeking more value. But what will 'value' be in the future? And what value will humans bring to service?

So glad you asked. Read on to find out about 5D Service!

Part 2

UNPACKING 5D SERVICE

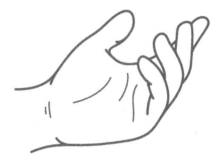

4. 5D SERVICE EXPLAINED

Your employees want to shine more brightly, and your customers will be attracted to this. 5D Service is for genuinely customer-obsessed businesses and leaders who believe leading is serving.

Ultimately, the future of customer service is a fusion of technology and human touch. While advanced technologies enhance efficiency and accessibility, the human element remains crucial. But how well are we developing, strengthening or even simply recognising the human dimensions of service? It's time leaders become proficient in these dimensions, normalise them in their ways of working and engaging, and trust that meaningful interactions between humans will build lasting customer relationships.

There are many ways to reimagine service in your business, community and the world. What is important to know is that service is multidimensional because we humans are multidimensional. Seeing service with multiple lenses will give you and your team the soft skills to:

- make the leap from ordinary to extraordinary service
- upgrade the capacity and capability to remove the customer's pain or problem
- evolve any outdated service norms so you are confident and relevant to the people you serve.

The 5D framework exists to help you and your business navigate the future and avoid fading into a melting pot of mediocrity or, worse, being irrelevant. Let me introduce 5D Service.

5D Service is a multidimensional approach to serving humans that goes beyond the traditional aspects of caring for your people and customer care. It's a comprehensive way of delivering service that considers and invites an awareness of five key dimensions of the whole human being.

The term '5D' has been inspired by various psychology, sociology and anthropology disciplines that helped me relate to the multiple facets of human behaviour, cognition and social interactions.

The 5D framework is based on decades of observing, training, coaching and developing human-to-human interactions in workplaces and communities. Like scientists who study chimpanzees, I love exploring the evolution and transformation of human behaviour. Each time I step into a conference room, workshop or training room, I learn more about leaders' challenges with their teams and customers and the human skills that have been forgotten or, at the very least, underutilised, as well as the skills that are desperately needed. I meditate, write, speak and mentor on this topic every day, and with eyes wide open, I continually find ways of breaking down a behemoth challenge like transforming a service culture into bite-sized activities over time.

The 5 dimensions of 5D Service will help you create service excellence now and into the future.

What 5D Service is not

In many ways, when you look around, we appear to have normalised or, at the very least, become accustomed to mediocre service interactions. Either that, or we've fallen under some kind of spell.

Let me paint a picture for you; maybe this picture is familiar to you also? An ordinary day, a few errands and appointments to attend. I take a family member to a medical appointment, get on a flight, check in to my hotel at the other end, do some quick personal shopping across the road from the hotel, grab dinner with some colleagues and drop into a supermarket on the way back. Multiple interactions as a customer, and all of them below average and predictably underwhelming:

- **At the medical appointment:** We arrive for a scheduled check-up. The receptionist confirms our appointment, checks my family member in and directs them to the waiting area. The receptionist efficiently carries out the necessary administrative tasks but does not engage with me or my family member beyond this.
- **At the airline check-in desk:** I have a bag to check in for this trip. The self-service kiosk is not working. An airline staff member walks up to me and, without eye contact or a smile, asks for my boarding pass, overrides the self-service kiosk, prints the baggage tags and tags the luggage, all in silence. The interaction is minimal and solely focused on completing the transaction as quickly as possible.
- **At the hotel:** I arrive and queue at the front desk. With a half-smile, the receptionist asks for my name, verifies my booking,

provides the room key and briefly explains where the room is located. The process is quick and efficient but lacks any personal touch or attempt to understand if I have any special requirements or interests.

- **At the retail store:** I walk in with a particular product in mind. I go to the register to find a human, as I can't see anyone on the floor. I ask where the product is, and the staff's reaction to my product request is a look of disapproval. They point in a particular direction, leaving me doubting if this product is reputable and wondering if I said something I shouldn't had? I find the product. I no longer feel good about it, so I leave without making a purchase.

- **At the restaurant:** I arrive where my colleagues suggested they would be and eventually find them. I sit at the table and wait for several minutes before a waiter sees me and offers me a drink. The menu is accessible via a QR code, and we are asked to use this when we're ready to order. We order. There is no more service for what feels like an eternity as I drain my first glass of wine. The food arrives with a brief explanation of what has been placed on the table, and then they are off. 'Dump and run' would be an accurate description. There is no more service. Our bill arrives, and we are asked to leave a tip on a mobile payment machine that is (yep, you guessed it) dumped on the table. We all agree that the tip request is an insult – who would we be tipping and what for? We get up and leave; no one from the restaurant says goodbye or asks if we enjoyed the meal.

- **At the supermarket:** Well, let's just say, even I am not paying attention by now.

Just an ordinary day, and soooo many opportunities for these people to make me feel just a little bit valued, unique or important – yet I collapsed on my hotel-room bed thinking how beige and two-dimensional each of those service interactions were. No one did anything wrong and no one was offensive, but equally, no one honoured the whole human that I am beyond the product or service. There was nothing special about any of it.

And so, on we go. Each day is a lot like the last. Walking around the world under the illusion that we're serving people with what we think they need – and yet missing opportunities each day, in the ordinary interactions, to reinforce and honour each other.

We don't need to be part of a religion or commit to community service to feel connected, cared for and part of something bigger than ourselves. If we take a more holistic approach to ordinary service interactions, we are nurturing that deep need to feel we matter. As the saying goes (often attributed to philosopher and psychologist John Dewey), 'The deepest urge in human nature is the desire to feel important'.

Customer service delivered by humans has a point of difference that needs to be articulated clearly. That point of difference is this: we can see all of the person in front of us. Beyond the product or service that the customer has come for, what they really want out of this engagement is often something only another human can sense, only a human can tap into, and only a human can provide (even if they are unconscious of it).

What 5D Service is

There are 5 dimensions of 5D Service, and when they're inter-connected and integrated as a service framework, you start to see magic. It's the 'magic' that happens when all the pieces of a puzzle come together to reveal a complete picture – in this case, revealing a complete human being who is serving and another whole human being who is being served.

Magic is all about the experience. It's the wonder, the joy, the moment of 'I can't believe what I just saw'. That's why so many of us love magic shows, even though we know there's a logical explanation somewhere deep down.

5D Service helps you make the unseen seen, the illogical logical, and the intangible tangible. *Leading a culture using the 5D Service framework will change how your people work and how they serve.*

In essence, 5D Service is a perfected 'magic trick' that requires deep understanding and mastery to provide a seamless, all-encompassing experience that leaves people and your customers in awe. And as with any magic trick, you have to practise to make it look effortless and masterful.

So, what are the 5 dimensions of service? Take a look.

There is a hierarchy in taking care of people

If you're familiar with Maslow's 'Hierarchy of Needs', you'll see some similarities. Maslow suggested that some needs take precedence over others: the most basic needs are at the bottom and the more complex ones are at the top (Maslow, 1943).

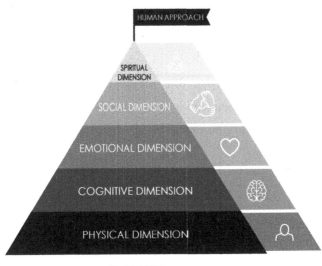

5D SERVICE

5D Service is also presented in a hierarchy, suggesting the correct order to look after people.

The most basic needs in service are at the bottom of the pyramid and the more complex ways to look after people are at the top.

1. **The physical dimension**, at the bottom of the pyramid, is what makes up the experience between two humans in a service exchange – it's the bodily gestures and senses used to approach, respond and act for the best communication in service.

2. **The cognitive dimension** is the thinking, rational aspect of service, helping you pay attention to the people you're serving and providing the decision-making skills needed to solve problems and be helpful in service.

3. **The emotional dimension** helps situational responses and allows people to see service as subjective. It involves understanding,

expressing and managing emotions, as well as empathising with others for engaging service.

4. **The social dimension** shapes our identity and gives us a sense of belonging through conversation for greater connection in service.

5. **The spiritual dimension** is the higher purpose and meaning – ensuring customers' unexpected needs are met by the service from employees.

The 5D Service framework acknowledges that individuals are complex and multi-faceted. To take the leap from ordinary to extraordinary service, we need to get good at understanding all 5 dimensions.

There are people all over the planet with a palpable need for connection, meaning and significance. The consequence of not having this human connection is remarkable. The CDC published a report that says social isolation increases a person's risk of premature death at a rate that rivals smoking, obesity and physical inactivity (CDC, n.d). Connection may be one of life's most important aspects; serving people is a direct vehicle for this. The era to lean in and believe, to behave and become the magnificent, intelligent and magical beings we are, in the everyday workplace serving ordinary people, is now. And if you and your teams are already operating at this level, then bravo! Let's do this together.

When you understand how to apply 5D Service in your world, you see why humans serve best.

5. THE PHYSICAL DIMENSION

Use your surroundings and your body to master communication in service

'Style is a way to say who you are without having to speak.'
—Rachel Zoe

My Nanna Joan was an Englishwoman who spoke like the Queen and drank tea like the Queen – in fact, I'm sure she thought she was the Queen (God rest her soul). An inspiring woman of her time, Nanna Joan was beautiful and had an eye for detail and quality. She taught me many things about manners, how I presented myself, how I spoke and pronounced my h's and, yes, how I drank tea. If Nanna Joan didn't like something I was wearing, she would simply say, in her very posh English accent, 'Always dress, darling, like you are about to meet the Queen'.

At worst, I would describe her as incredibly vain. At best, she was extremely proud of who she had become and always wanted to present her best self to the world. She taught me an important lesson: to always present yourself and your environment to give a positive impression because you never know who you'll meet or what opportunities (or challenges) the day may bring.

What impression does your 'shop window' give?

When you walk into a space for the first time, what do you notice straight away? What impressions are being made by the physical space that surrounds you?

The waiting room of a doctor's surgery. A shopping centre. An airline check-in area. The reception area of an office space. A company's website. Your very own desk area. These are all 'shop windows', giving the first impressions of who you are as a business and what messages you want your customers and stakeholders to receive about your brand.

Your business's 'shop window' offers your first opportunity to be notable and to create a positive impression that gives you a head start on creating a competitive advantage. A well-presented and well-maintained physical environment showcases your brand's values, culture and professionalism. It sends a message to clients, competitors and employees about the calibre and standards of your business. The same applies to an online experience, where the surroundings are virtual.

The physical dimension of service can set the stage for a positive experience even before any service interaction takes place. An environment can also facilitate or discourage interactions. When your spaces are cleverly thought out and designed with the customer who uses that space in mind, you can influence people's behaviour. For example, an inviting waiting room with comfortable chairs and privacy in a hospital can encourage people to visit a patient for longer. An office space can be designed to foster creativity, productivity and wellbeing.

The physical environment is the most tangible, practical and easiest place to start elevating your service reputation, so get it right. Non-negotiable. I cannot stand a dirty toilet. Lights that don't turn on. A cold room. Music that makes me anxious. Smells that are, well . . . unpleasant. A confusing website. An endless, frustrating phone menu. This is low-hanging fruit.

So, get your space right. Walk through it like you're a customer for the first time. Call your help hotline. Visit your website. The environment sets the tone for the staff and their internal and external interactions, helping shape the experience from the very beginning.

Enough said. Just do it, and let's move on to the trickier part of the physical dimension: humans.

Having a body is a service advantage

One of the things that makes us human is that we have physical bodies. When you have humans in any physical space providing service, they can influence other people's experience simply by how they present themselves and the way they move.

Nonverbal information is being communicated through many channels of your body, including facial expressions, how you walk, orientate your body, your physical posture, your eye gaze and movements, and your hand gestures. You can hold entire conversations and exchange critical information without saying a word.

Of course, the physical dimension of service also incorporates using our senses and motor skills to complete tasks and be helpful. But dress code, body language and professional demeanour can instil confidence and trust in customers before exchanging words.

The physical dimension can tell the external world that your company values its people and strives for excellence.

I was reminded of this recently when I visited the theatre to watch a fabulous musical, *& Juliet*. In a city like Melbourne, we're spoilt for choice with theatres, and I hadn't been to the Regent Theatre before. It is incredibly stunning and ornate, with tall ceilings, acoustically designed walls and great seating – really comfy leather seats with cool pockets for your belongings (picture business-class seats on a plane). As soon as I walked in, my excitement and anticipation were heightened. They had the 'shop window' – the physical surroundings – absolutely nailed.

Consider the impression I got when the orchestra began tuning their instruments in the orchestra pit. The musicians' formal attire, poise and focus on their work suggested a seriousness and dedication to their craft. Their visible and audible preparation also built anticipation. The musical hadn't started yet, but the stage was set, and my expectations rose again. All without words or an exchange with another human being, based on observations of how the space and staff were presented.

Your body has powerful ways of getting across information. Humans can sense a friend or foe in 7 seconds, and we decide whether we trust and respect a person just based on how they move their body. Your body can portray confidence and strength to another person without whispering a word. The way you move can communicate positive messages to people and help diffuse negative situations.

Knowing that your body is crucial in creating a first impression on other humans is vital in service. In her book *Presence*, Amy Cuddy (a Harvard psychologist who spent 15 years studying first impressions) states that people answer two basic questions that determine whether they like you and want to conduct business with you during a first impression:

1. Can I trust this person?
2. Can I respect this person? (Cuddy, 2015)

Your body might sometimes be described as having a mind of its own. Truth is, your mind is in every cell of your body, and your emotions are stored in your body. The body isn't just there to carry around your brain.

And your body is unique – made up of approximately 37 trillion cells, expressing your genetic code, a code that no other animal or machine has. Or as the brilliant dancer Martha Graham put it, 'There is a vitality, a life force, a quickening that is translated through you into action, and there is only one of you in all time, this expression is unique, and if you block it, it will never exist through any other medium; and be lost' (Graham, in De Mille, 1992).

When you are in tune with your body during service interactions, you will be more alive, more creative, and more authentic. And the people you are serving will feel that.

The most obvious place to start elevating the value of humans in customer service is to upgrade our physical abilities.

Become more ninja-like

From the day I stepped into the workplace, I was told about the concept of open body language. If you've done any reading or training in soft skills or how to make positive impressions, you're probably familiar with it. Keep your arms and legs uncrossed and your hands open; turn your face, torso, legs and feet towards the other person, and have an open, receptive facial expression. In the context of communicating and relating to people, gestures, postures and mannerisms are what make interactions more effective.

Open body language has been helpful up until now. But in the digital era and for the future of service, it's a good starting point, but nowhere near enough to create trust and intimacy. The future asks us to be far more resourceful with our bodies and how we move them. We need to be more like ninjas.

Ninjas are trained to gather information. From an early age, they are trained to be incredibly aware of their surroundings, listen with all their senses and walk and move quietly but with precision. They learn skills that enable them to pop up in the most unlikely places. Their physical training maintains their bodies to ensure they have a level of flexibility so they can bend and move stealthily through difficult terrain. They also use technology and secret codes to support their missions.

Maybe you've never read much about ninjas, but perhaps you've heard of the famous American media franchise Teenage Mutant Ninja Turtles? My middle brother and I got swept up in the world of the Ninja Turtles with their super-cool, punky, easy-going demeanour. Us Gen Xers were captivated by their streetwise ways of conquering evil in New York City. The jingle, 'Heroes in a half shell, Turtle Power', still rings in my head.

Leonardo, Michelangelo, Donatello and Raphael were four anthropomorphic turtle brothers trained in ninjutsu and possessed meta-human abilities like enhanced strength, speed, agility and reflexes. They were irresistible to us. I'm sure my brother thought he was the fifth turtle brother at one point, believing he could do superhuman things, flying off the couch and jumping down flights of stairs ready for whatever mission was in his imaginative head! Still, it's a useful model for humans serving on the frontline in the future. Become more ninja-like: upgrade your open body language to Ninja Turtle skills.

Mastering the physical dimension of service is to create seamless, fluid, effortless interpersonal exchanges, sort of like when a ninja is moving from point A to B. You know they're there; you feel their presence. Yet, they're not overwhelmingly dominant in the space; they move with precision, focus, intention and grace. You sense they're ready to serve the moment you indicate you need them. Simply by how they move their body, you feel confident in their ability to help you, creating trust.

If we want to be more aware of our physical surroundings, more prepared for any mission that comes our way, and more choreo-graphed with how we use our body, we need to be more ninja-like. We need to bring more Turtle Power!

At the time of writing this, I was in a very popular restaurant in downtown San Francisco. I watched a robot move around the restau-rant floor, clearing tables and stacking plates. It was efficient, but the opportunity to glance and make eye contact, see my gesture for another beverage, smile at me or indicate gratitude for my custom was lost. For humans to serve best, we must use our unique bodies as an advantage over any machine solution.

There are plenty of techniques that ServiceQ teaches service professionals to help them master the physical dimension, but for now, let's start with these three simple ones:

1. Take responsibility for your self-care practices; this era of stress and burnout places pressure on your body.
2. Wake up your five senses. Society is making it harder for people to feel their full range of senses and, therefore, to feel fully alive.
3. Upgrade your ideas about open body language and realise the powerful intelligence of your body and how mastering your gestures can make communication flow.

A snapshot of how to master the physical dimension

POINTS OF FAILURE	KEYS TO OVERCOMING	EXAMPLE TECHNIQUE
Not at home in your body; struggle to maintain health	Prioritise your health, move in ways you enjoy	Ninja self-care practices
Tuned out, numb	Tuned in, alert	Wake up your five senses
Open body language is not enough	Use your body as a communication tool	Master your gestures

Technique 1: Ninja self-care practices

Service roles are challenging at the best of times, and some are physically demanding. To give your body a fighting chance at supporting you in everyday life, you must look after it – especially if you want to communicate with power and purpose through your body.

Looking after yourself physically may mean different things to different people; however, the goal is to have your body working at its optimum to stay fit and well. Health is multi-faceted, so self-care must be as well.

Here are some obvious physical practices that will keep you moving with speed, strength, flexibility and agility, as well as supporting your nervous system during times of stress or heavy workload:

- Attending health upkeep appointments (GP, massage, acupuncture, chiropractic, kinesiology, etc.). These can help you stay in tune with your body, get ahead of potential problems, or just relax and enjoy some care.
- Resting when unwell. Don't come into work, and certainly don't serve people when you're unwell. The best thing you can do is stay away, heal and return when you're well again.
- Drinking enough water.
- Getting sufficient sleep.
- Eating regular meals and a healthy diet.
- Exercising outdoors.
- Enjoying group exercise.
- Maintaining good hygiene.
- Keeping your environment clean, tidy and free of toxins and clutter.

The trend of workplaces and employers taking more responsibility for their employees' health and wellbeing is admirable. Still, ultimately, you will always be best at taking good care of yourself. When you do, it sends a message to your customers that you can take good care of them too!

Technique 2: Wake up your five senses!

To appreciate the physical world, we must recognise that seeing, hearing, smelling, tasting and feeling is truly a gift. The five senses are our window on reality. Many humans are only opening their senses ever so slightly – we don't always see the complete picture. And that's okay at times. The world can be difficult, so it can be helpful to shut down our senses sometimes. Sensory experiences are so powerful that some people can feel overwhelmed. In many stadiums and public gathering areas, a sensory room is necessary – a place to give people a break from the potential overstimulation of a mass gathering.

Having said that, the five senses are one of those superpowers that are underutilised in human-to-human interactions to increase our perception of others. If you often wonder why you're not very perceptive or feel that your awareness of what's happening around you is limited, you need to wake up your five senses.

Our senses are a special human feature that robots and computers don't have. They spark feelings and allow us to appreciate beauty and experience wonder. They enable us to constantly gather information and act on this intelligence. You might see a customer distressed or in need. You might realise a fellow employee is worried by listening to the tone of their voice. You could be enjoying a concert and feel a sense of connection with the crowd. You are constantly receiving insights and important cues through your five senses. How often do you value and act on this information? Will our human senses become even more valuable as more and more day-to-day tasks are completed by machines?

We must place a much higher value on our senses and see our bodies as instruments. Musicians often use a tuning fork to tune musical instruments. In the same way, our bodies need tuning from time to time to create a clear channel to receive everything our senses can reveal. To tune up your sensory awareness, add the following five senses activity to your daily routine: at the start of your day, the beginning of your shift or a mini-break at lunchtime.

The Five Senses exercise

Pause and do a body scan. Unclench your jaw. Relax your shoulders. Take a deep breath.

1. **Notice five things you can see.** Pick something you don't usually notice, like a shadow or a small crack in the concrete.
2. **Notice four things you can feel.** Bring awareness to four things you are currently feeling, like the texture of your clothing or the breeze on your skin.
3. **Notice three things you can hear.** Take a moment to listen to and note three things you can hear in the background. This could be the hum of a refrigerator, the faint sound of traffic nearby or a bird chirping.
4. **Notice two things you can smell.** Bring your awareness to smells you usually filter out, whether pleasant or unpleasant.
5. **Notice one thing you can taste.** Focus on one thing you can taste right now in this moment. You can take a sip of a drink or even open your mouth and notice anything you can taste in the air.

Technique 3: Master your gestures

Gestures are one part of open body language humans must master to serve best. I don't think I fully appreciated how powerful gestures were until I started travelling the world in places I couldn't communicate with words. In India, Asia and Europe, I realised that language was more than what came out of your mouth. It's also

about when to be light and when to be serious, when to show gratitude and when to reference tradition. The more you observe and
practise the art of gesturing, the better you communicate. Studies
have shown that people unconsciously look for congruence between
speech and gestures to determine whether they can trust you. And
people who gesture more are frequently judged to be warmer than
those who don't. Researchers who analysed the most viral TED Talks
found that the speakers gestured twice as much as their less-popular
counterparts. So, gestures are pretty powerful!

Your gestures are like a second language that you can use to
emphasise an important point, show that you are listening intently,
or signal that you have a question. Being proficient in gestures is
a wonderful skill for life – and mastering gestures is expected in
service. Paying attention to other people's gestures (and your own)
dials up your awareness of what people are telling you, intentionally
or otherwise. Using your own body language more consciously will
instantly elevate your level of service.

If you can't jump on a plane, people-watching close to home is a
great place to observe and begin building your gesture vocabulary.
When you closely observe people interacting in meetings, with colleagues in the workplace and in service interactions, you'll realise
that their gestures are (often unconscious) expressions of what's
happening in their minds. The better you understand your customers
and colleagues, the easier it is to serve them well. Gestures offer a
little sprinkling of magic in service. They're uniquely human and can
accelerate the building of trust and respect between you and the
person you're serving tenfold. I could write a whole book on this
subject – many people have. Still, for the purposes of this book, I will

keep the concept of 'gestures' narrow and focused. Let's look just at hand gestures, head gestures and eye movements.

To build on the basics of open body language, master the gestures in the following three tables. Make these non-negotiable; if you do the things in the 'Master' columns each time you interact with humans, you'll be well on your way to mastering communication and creating healthier relationships.

Hand and arm gestures

Avoid	Master
Clenched fists (not relaxed, angry)	Palms open and facing up (relaxed and calm)
Crossed arms (closed off to the conversation)	Arms open (open to the conversation)
Hands in pockets (uninterested and disengaged)	Hands out and away from the body (engaged and interested)
Fidgeting and pointing fingers or waving hands above the head (not focused and not paying attention)	Staying still (a focused and competent professional)

Head gestures

Avoid	Master
Turning your head away from the other person (not listening)	Turning your head to face the person directly (listening)
Stunned head, no movement (not listening)	Tilting your head to the side when listening, exposing one of your ears (listening) Nodding your head to show you agree or understand (listening to understand)

Eye gaze and movement

Avoid	Master
No eye contact (shy or untrustworthy)	Maintaining eye contact throughout the conversation or interaction (confident and trustworthy)
Staring at the other person (arrogant and domineering)	Alternating your gaze every 5 to 10 seconds (confident and friendly)

These gestures may vary from culture to culture, of course. For example, nodding or shaking one's head might not be understood as 'yes' or 'no' in the same way in one culture as another. Understanding cultural nuances in nonverbal communication is essential – it pays to spend some time exploring the various cultures of your team and customers.

A special call-out to anyone reading this who spends a lot of time working with people through digital channels – communicating over the phone, email or live chat. Please don't disregard this element of the physical dimension! Mastering your gestures will help you and the people on the receiving end of your service. For example, smiling while on the phone, staying still while serving a customer via live chat and nodding your head to indicate you agree and understand when speaking will translate into your communication and be felt by the listener. For a deeper dive into digital body language, I'll point you towards a fabulous book written just for people in roles like yours: Erica Dhawan's *Digital Body Language*. It's crammed with ideas and ways to translate trust and connection with people, no matter the distance.

So, now you have a few starting points to help you build a solid base for your 5D Service pyramid. Let's move to the next level: the cognitive dimension.

6. THE COGNITIVE DIMENSION

Pay attention and process information to be helpful in service

'One machine can do the work of fifty ordinary men.
No machine can do the work of one extraordinary man.'
—Elbert Hubbard

Have we forgotten how smart we are? Have we forgotten the power of the mind and its unique ability to see problems and people through various perspectives? Have we given our thinking and processing power over to the machines entirely?

Our default idea for improving service appears to now be, 'AI will solve this problem'. But what if humans realised that we are the highest technology on the planet, and we can problem-solve beyond any machine if we learn to master our minds?

Don't fight the mind; use it to get present

Think back to when you were served by someone who wasn't entirely with you – they were there in body but their mind was someplace else.

Years ago, I did an experiment: I had a hidden camera on me and hit the streets to paint a picture of the subtleties of being served by someone present and someone who is not. The video captured a very innocent moment. I had given the barista my name when ordering my latte. When it came time to collect my drink, the same barista looked me straight in the eye and handed me 'my order', calling me Hamish. Wrong name, wrong order.

Being present is one of the most precious gifts we can give another human being. This is true in both professional and personal relationships. To create healthy relationships in life, you must be present with people.

Let's say you're telling your partner a story at the dinner table, and they seem distracted. They're not making eye contact with you and their thoughts appear elsewhere. How do their vacant eyes make you feel as you tell your story? Maybe you feel invisible or that what you say isn't important. It appears the voice in your partner's head has their attention, not you. Not paying attention and being fully present with people is one of the quickest ways to damage relationships. The more present we are, the better we can use our minds to strengthen relationships, whether with strangers or friends.

Our minds are exquisitely designed with trillions of neuron connections. This is why we're so creative and innovative – and why the skills of critical thinking, problem-solving and being helpful to others are uniquely human and in high demand in the workplace.

Most problems in the workplace and problems associated with customer service are really just situations; our relationship to these situations and the quality of our thinking makes a situation a problem. When we learn to master the mind, we learn to master problem-solving, which makes us incredibly helpful in service and in life.

I was drawn to this quote in a McKinsey newsletter, 'Mind the Gap' (11 April 2023):

> '. . . an indispensable skill in this brave new world is critical thinking. It's "purposeful, reasonable, and reflective thinking when you are faced with complex issues and conflicting situations." That includes probing and questioning assumptions, gathering info, and putting it all together into a well-reasoned argument.'
>
> (Hilton Segel & Hatami 2023)

The cognitive dimension of 5D Service is not about your thoughts; **it's about your ability to utilise your thoughts and technology within, and apply the mental faculties of attention, intention, focus, curiosity and diligence in human-to-human interaction.**

Those who are most present with the person in front of them are most helpful in service. When you're present, you can access those mental faculties. Without these faculties, however, your problem-solving or helpfulness in a service environment will be only as good as a machine's. But we are so much greater than machines. We created them, don't forget!

When a human uses the cognitive dimension to its fullest capacity, it creates extraordinary moments for people.

An airport maintenance worker called Joel spoke up in one ServiceQ training webinar, sharing a story with colleagues from all over the airport community about a lost traveller who needed directions for the airport hotel. He explained that he could tell that English was their second language, so rather than point to a landmark or show directions on a map, he walked the traveller to the hotel himself. Using your words and feet to help someone in a service situation is a uniquely human approach and an excellent example of humans serving best by using their whole brains to think and solve problems. During that walk and time together, Joel and the traveller shared some banter in broken English and a few laughs. They created a connection that went far beyond solving a problem.

Often, customers and people in your care are just looking for someone to make sense of a situation – someone who will pay attention so that they can read the whole picture and be helpful.

To be brilliant critical thinkers, problem-solvers and helpful humans at work, people need to dial up their awareness of when they are present and when they are not.

When you're not present, it's like living in a forest without seeing any trees. But you can't overlook the forest and only focus on the trees. You need to see both, to expand and contract your points of view, and zoom in and zoom out and see the whole picture. To do this, you must be present.

The techniques to maintain a level of presence and exercise the whole brain are endless. For now, let's look at three techniques that anyone in service can practise immediately.

A snapshot of the cognitive dimension

POINTS OF FAILURE	KEYS TO OVERCOMING	EXAMPLE TECHNIQUE
You get distracted	Pay attention	Undivided attention
You lack confidence in decision-making	Sensible awareness and thinking systems	Use common sense
Your thinking is narrow	Curiosity and critical thinking	Ask questions to solve the right problems

Technique 1: Undivided attention

As I said before, computers and robots may be able to turn a camera and look at you, but they can't pay attention. When you think about what being present looks like in action, one of the ways it could be described is 'giving someone your undivided attention'. The opposite of this is dividing your focus – putting your attention in multiple places simultaneously. When this takes place, we are likely to be distracted.

One of the most magnificent superpowers of being human is that we can focus our attention. We can turn our attention on and off based on whether we're interested in something. And when we're not interested in something, we struggle to focus on it. The point is that you kind of need to be a little interested in humans and how they behave and act if you want half a chance of giving them your undivided attention.

For some people, holding attention is a real challenge; for others, providing undivided attention to a task or human is their point of difference, making them high performers and a threat to their competitors.

One of the greatest practices for building sharper concentration and clarity of thought, being able to return to the present moment more often throughout the day, is meditation.

My personal journey with meditation has healed my previous addiction to always wanting to think, worry about and live in the future. As a highly conscientious planner and goal-focused individual, I allowed my mind to hang out more in the future than in the now. This manifested in anxiety, which was debilitating for many years.

Meditation has completely resolved my previous issues of anxiety and panic attacks, and I've become dedicated to a meditation practice that keeps me more in the present moment instead of the future. It's helped me move through the world with a little less suffering – and the bonus was its profound impact on the people around me, too!

Tim Ferriss has one of the world's most popular podcasts (*The Tim Ferriss Show*), and his book *Tools of Titans* summarises tools and tactics used by world-class performers, billionaires and entrepreneurs. It turns out that 80 per cent of these billionaires, world-class athletes, famous performers and business icons credit meditation practice as instrumental to their success (Ferriss, 2016).

Meditation is a daily Service Habit that ServiceQ has been teaching employees across all job roles and industries to help support them in their busy workplaces. You can read more about meditation and how it specifically supports service in Chapter 5 of the *Service Habits* (2nd ed.) book. I created an online audio program called '66 Days of Meditation' to give you a head start. You can download it here – https://jaquiescammell.com/66-days-of-meditation – and practise just 10 minutes a day to stabilise and strengthen the mind.

Technique 2: Use common sense

Over the past decade, I've been asked multiple times, 'Can you teach people common sense?' This request comes from the frustrated leaders of service professionals who are missing obvious clues and cues when serving.

Too much intellectualism can run us over. It's essential to bring some sensible awareness of which service solutions are practical and reasonable for a person's situation. Often, service professionals miss the mark because they've allowed their cleverness to overshadow their humanness. We need to always weigh up the logic and the emotion of a situation and make decisions from there. Those who serve best are those people who can see the whole picture – not just to consider data, rules and logic, but also to consider feelings, values and sensible reason.

Common sense can feel less tangible because it's often used when you're without all the information or data. Still, it's the action that feels wise. It's like a compass. It may not give you every detail of the terrain ahead, but it always points you in the right direction. This is perhaps why some people find it hard to teach common sense. We're wired to look at all the details rather than to trust our intuition or deep knowing that the direction we're heading doesn't make sense, doesn't feel right, and that there is a whisper asking you to zoom out and see this situation with a different lens rather than letting cleverness get in the way.

Humans will always serve best in the digital era when we use our unique ability to understand what other humans may be thinking. Common sense is often based on a unique capacity of human beings, developed in the brain when we are young, called the 'theory of mind'. In simple terms, it's where you realise that other people have different information than you. Humans have a theory of mind, so we can be far more proactive and powerful in problem-solving. Our ability to apply reasoning to determine what might be going on for another person is advantageous.

You can teach people common sense if you teach them how the mind works and to genuinely try to understand what other human beings are thinking. One simple exercise ServiceQ teaches will help you remember that other people don't think like you, and to access some common sense is to ask a simple (silent) question, 'What's it like to be you?' Immediately, this question creates curiosity and objectivity, allowing you to see things through a different lens. The hardest part of this exercise is remembering to do it!

Technique 3: Ask questions to solve the right problems

The very nature of our mind compels us to wonder why things are the way they are. The more questions we ask, the better we can understand people and solve the right problems.

I recently cancelled a dinner at a hotel I was staying at. I spoke to the lady at the front desk and simply said, 'I'd like to cancel dinner tonight'. The look on her face and the awkward pause were the non-verbal cues that she needed an explanation as to why I was cancelling. The interaction between her and I could have been a shallow transactional experience, but it wasn't. It became a conversation fuelled by curiosity and intrigue. The employee learned more about me and why I wanted to cancel dinner, which made me feel cared for and allowed her to offer alternatives to my dinner that I hadn't considered.

The more we ask why, the more we ask for further information. The more we ask great questions, the more we learn, and the better we can pre-empt and provide alternatives to those we serve.

Sure, a learning machine will keep learning, but it will only ask why if it's been programmed to; it's less interested in understanding and more focused on getting you an outcome. My simple understanding of coding machines is that you give the computer the goal, a specific outcome. *But service is subjective and often defined by the process, not the outcome.* It's understanding the other person's point of view, showing them, through great questions and empathy, that you care about them, and seeking all alternatives before landing on a solution. There are endless resources on this technique in the second edition of my *Service Habits* book to get started or build greater muscle in crafting your questions. But for a quick tip, remember the golden rule of asking questions: **Ask questions that create a conversation.** Using open questions that start with 'who', 'what', 'why', 'when', 'where' and 'how' is a great place to start.

Yes, AI is great for efficiencies and quick information and solutions in today's world; however, our human need to know why or learn more about something is why humans serve best. This intellectual curiosity brings out the best solutions for humanity: we get to the core of a problem and don't simply transact.

In the McKinsey article 'Author Talks', author, chief innovation officer, and professor Tomas Chamorro-Premuzic, highlights that sometimes asking the right questions can be more important than the answers. Businesses and technologists are focusing on making AI smarter and better; he asks:

'What should we be doing now that we have created technologies, machines, and computers that can do all these things? [. . .] I don't know the definitive answer to this question, but I can tell you it's probably not staring at your screen or phone for most of your day, clicking on boxes, and reacting to algorithmic recommendations to train AI to get even better.'

(Chamorro-Premuzic, 2023)

Remember, the better we are at solving problems, the more we grow as a species. As Tony Robbins has been famously quoted to say: 'Every problem is a gift – without problems we would not grow'.

7. THE EMOTIONAL DIMENSION

Understand and balance emotions to give engaging service

*'Illusions commend themselves to us because they
save us pain and allow us to enjoy pleasure instead.'*
—Sigmund Freud

I regularly drive about 80 kilometres to a small town in regional Victoria for kinesiology. In simple terms, my kinesiologist uses hands-on therapy to help me release trapped emotions and subconscious memories that can impact my health and my performance. It's often the emotional shit that needs some unlocking. As Sigmund Freud once said, 'Unexpressed emotions will never die. They are buried alive and will come forth later in uglier ways'.

I share this little bit about me to introduce the emotional dimension of service. Because to better understand other people's emotions, you first need to understand your own and how to work with them. The ability to feel and sense emotions in others is another incredible advantage of being human and serving others. *Service is recognising how people feel and then aiming to make them feel better.*

The emotional dimension involves the examination of our human emotions and how they impact others – aka the feelings stuff. It's the

ability to go beyond an awareness of our emotional state and introduce a layer that enables us to empathise and act from a place of
understanding and compassion.

In any relationship – at work, home or in the community – the
better we understand the emotions that drive our thoughts, attitudes
and experiences, the better our relationships become.

Feeling emotions

The intriguing 2020 documentary *The Social Dilemma* had many
key messages about how social media has changed and continues to
change how people behave and act. One that has stayed with me
is how humans are described in the social media galaxy as 'users'.
Edward Tufte, a computer scientist and professor emeritus at Yale,
stated that only two industries call their customers 'users': the illegal
drug industry and the software industry.

A machine will treat humans as a 'user', and while machines can
be set up to understand how the 'user' behaves, they don't necessarily
know how we feel.

Creating an emotional connection is a uniquely human gift we
need to better understand and leverage to provide outstanding
service. To feel emotion is to be fully alive and awake to all our
incredible human potential. However, not everyone has the willing-
ness and the tools to notice how they are feeling from moment to
moment and how those feelings drive their interactions with other
people. When we're unaware of our own emotions, we can find work
and life difficult. People may misunderstand us, and we may mis-
interpret others' intentions or actions.

All of our emotions are a part of being human. The pain and the pleasure. The ones we run away from and avoid and the ones we run towards and desire. Denying an emotion within you is denying a part of you. Derek Sivers, in his book *How to live*, says:

> *'If you over protect yourself from pain, then every little challenge will feel unbearably difficult.*
> *People say they're not doing the work because it's hard.*
> *But it's hard because they're not doing the work.'*
> (Sivers, 2021)

Sivers has a point. Feeling uncomfortable emotions is easier said than done; many people have become masters at numbing their emotions to avoid pain.

When we're unwilling to sit with uncomfortable emotions, we eventually lose the skill of self-regulating and dealing with emotions. To recognise other people's emotions, particularly at work, you must first allow yourself to feel them.

Here's a way to quietly test this concept for yourself. Recall a time when someone approached you to challenge your work, or you were the first port of call for someone to complain to more generally. How did you feel? How well were you able to sit with that feeling? If the answer is that it didn't feel great and you noticed that you wanted to run away, deflect the feeling, or you started to spiral into overwhelm, then maybe your emotional fitness requires some training.

As Susan David points out in her book *Emotional Agility*, emotionally intelligent people who self-regulate well through stressful or uncomfortable situations have not been gifted a special gene from nature. They continually do the inner work of learning to sit with and make friends with all types of feelings (David, 2016).

The more 'friendly' we become with a full range of emotions – from anger to ecstasy – the more prepared we are for the big, strong, challenging emotions others will project onto us. Want to be more resilient? Get curious about your emotions and how they move, ebb and flow.

Balancing emotions

I was always raised to be kind to people regardless of your feelings. If you needed a minute, you'd take a quiet, private moment to let the feeling pass. Yes, to feel the emotion until it passed. This wasn't about denying my feelings but rather about not being constantly swept up in powerful emotional currents that might make a difficult situation harder to navigate.

Growing up on the North Coast of NSW, Australia, I experienced this teaching on a profoundly physical level. Because we all spent so much time at the beach, it was part of our school curriculum to learn basic surf lifesaving skills like reading the surf and navigating a rip. The surf lifesaving teacher explained how important it was not to swim against the rip, even if we were instinctively frightened of being dragged out into deeper water. The teacher explained that if we swam against the rip, we'd quickly become exhausted, and our chances of drowning would be much higher. Instead, we needed to go with the rip and trust that it would eventually lose its power and we would be able to swim safely back to shore.

The more we ignore, resist or suppress our internal emotional world, the more it feels like we're fighting a powerful riptide and drowning despite our best efforts. But even the most powerful riptide of emotions loses its power. This too, shall pass.

Another way to think about it is that we're turning towards our emotional experience instead of away from it. When we do:

- we handle challenges and changes with greater ease and calmness instead of waiting for the external world to change
- our relationships improve because feeling and flowing with our own 'inner riptides' helps us become more understanding and compassionate when we experience someone struggling with an overwhelming emotion.

Reading emotions

The human ability to read emotions is like radar that skilfully catches reflected energy from an object. When we hone our inner radar, we can perceive the emotional energy of others and understand the internal emotional states that might be driving the behaviours we observe.

If someone points at you and raises their voice, you'll guess that these behaviours suggest they're feeling the emotions of frustration and anger. If someone stares vacantly at you, eyes wide open, and is moving with caution, you'll guess their behaviours suggest that they are feeling lost or confused. And it is a guess. No one ever really knows how another person feels. Still, the more we study and observe people, the better our guesses become.

So, where do you go to study people and improve your emotional radar'?

If I go back to my McDonald's days in the 1980s and 90s, customer service was critical to each Big Mac-and-fries purchase. The 'soft skills' used to reinforce quality service interactions included the smile, using names, practising empathy and the ability to deal with ambiguity – aka customer complaints.

Serving thousands of humans in person, face-to-face and witnessing strong emotions at times provided us with incredible training in human behaviour and understanding what ethical treatment of people looked like in action (particularly in the drive-thru when people had to wait more than 3 minutes for their cheeseburger!).

The regular faces, the people dining alone, the family traditions such as children's treat nights and kids' birthday parties – the Port Macquarie McDonald's dining room gave me a snapshot of society. As a result, the other staff and I learned to recognise all sorts of human needs. In the first chapter of our working lives, we teenagers built emotional fitness through experiencing humanity dining in a fast-food restaurant.

Without face-to-face interactions in service, we lose a critical training ground for humans to learn how to read emotions. At what point do our efficiencies cost us the human qualities we need to fully experience ourselves and others? Are we sacrificing too much of our humanity for productivity and profits?

Our society is delicate, and it's our relationships that will keep it strong and healthy – if we have a healthy relationship with our emotions. We need to learn to self-regulate. And nowhere is this skill more critical than in service.

Being a valuable member of society, business or in a team involves being able to recognise emotions in others and act to serve the other person's needs, not your own. The way we read other people and respond to them reinforces the values that we each have, and it also supports that each of us has a stake in the other. Emotional agility is the key to fulfilling relationships with ourselves, others and the world around us.

There are many ways to dive into emotional agility and learn practices that improve it in work and life. I'd like to introduce to you three techniques that are crucial in service environments.

A snapshot of how to embody the emotional dimension

POINTS OF FAILURE	KEYS TO OVERCOMING	EXAMPLE TECHNIQUE
Quit when emotions get uncomfortable (yours or other people's)	Emotional regulating	Expand your emotional vocabulary
Guess other people's feelings	Recognise emotion in other people	Phrasing and questions
Irrational behaviour	Behavioural flexibility	Recognise your no-go behaviours

Technique 1: Expand your emotional vocabulary

As intelligent machines take over more repetitive and basic tasks, humans must provide the emotional aspect of service interactions. This involves understanding and managing your emotions and empathising with other people's emotions.

Dialling up your emotional vocabulary and getting skilled at noticing and naming emotions is a great place to start building emotional regulation. Labelling emotions creates objectivity and space between yourself and your feelings. In serving others, finding various words for emotions and different ways of expressing them for yourself and those you serve will accelerate your ability to empathise with people.

Step 1: Notice it

This first step is to become aware of your emotional state in the present moment. This allows you to pause and observe your emotions to respond appropriately rather than react unconsciously. What feelings or sensations do you notice in your body?

Step 2: Name it

Give the feeling or emotion a name. Be as specific as you can. Is it frustration? Anger? Perhaps it's sadness? Or surprise? If you can't put your finger on emotion-specific terminology, you could choose a sound such as 'ugh' or 'yay' to name the emotion or even give it a name such as 'Fred'. This will make that feeling easier to identify in future and allow you to clearly distinguish it from other emotions.

Simple tip

Get a list of emotions and feelings together that can become a reference point for expanding your vocabulary. If you search for 'list of emotions' online, you'll find names for various shades and tones of emotions that you perhaps don't use often but may be more appropriate, or you feel fit in future conversations.

For example, if I want to show empathy to someone I sense is frustrated, other words that may fit the scenario could be 'annoyed', 'aggravated', 'dismayed', disgruntled', 'displeased' or 'irritated'.

Technique 2: Phrasing and questions

To improve your 'guesswork' in reading other people's emotions, it's vital to ask questions and use phrases that draw out information and help you find out what's really going on for the other person. This is particularly helpful when:

- you have to tell someone (colleague or customer) bad news
- you're dealing with a complaint
- the other person has hidden disabilities, such as mental-health issues or partial hearing loss
- you're dealing with diverse cultures and languages.

The goal is to gain insight into the person's feelings. Pay attention to their tone of voice, their choice of words and how they're physically moving their body – their gestures and facial expressions.

As with your emotional vocabulary, building your list of helpful questions and phrases is useful. Try some of the following to dig a little deeper and test your assumptions about what another person is experiencing:

- 'You sound quite upset about this issue. Would you like to tell me more about what happened?'
- 'It seems like you're quite pleased with our service. What did you find most satisfying?'
- 'I sense some hesitation in your voice. Is there something you're concerned about?'
- 'I notice that you're asking a lot of detailed questions. Are you feeling unsure about this decision?'

- 'It sounds like you're frustrated with the process. Could you help me understand exactly what's causing this frustration?'
- 'Your excitement is contagious! What about our product/service excites you the most?'
- 'I sense a bit of confusion. What can I clarify for you?'
- 'You seem a bit quiet today. Is there something on your mind that you'd like to discuss?'
- 'You've mentioned a few times that this is important for you. Can you tell me more about why it's so significant?'
- 'You seem relieved. Were you worried about the outcome of this situation?'

Technique 3: Recognise your no-go behaviours

Recognising your 'no-go' behaviours will strengthen your behavioural flexibility: your ability to change your behaviours to respond to the changing environment around you, including those in that environment.

Most of the clients ServiceQ helps seek greater behavioural flexibility. The service transformation programs we deliver allow people in the workplace to bend and flex their behaviour through scenarios, different customer personas and situational examples: to work out when to step forward; when to step back; when to confidently say yes; when to ask for help; when to listen more intently; when to paraphrase; when to speak loudly; when to use silence; when to be more assertive; and when to stand still and smile.

A great place to start building behavioural flexibility is to get familiar with your uncomfortable feelings. Reflect on these questions:

- How comfortable are you with feeling uncomfortable?
- Which emotions do you turn towards, and which do you turn away from?
- What actions or behaviours do you know you don't do or would rather ask someone else to take care of?

You may see a correlation between the emotions you avoid and the behaviours you're unlikely to do – your no-go behaviours. For example, if you're uncomfortable with positive, happy people, you may find it hard to smile and act in a way that reflects a positive and happy vibe yourself. If you're uncomfortable with loud and assertive people, you may find it hard to speak loudly and give direction when a situation requires it.

The times when we need resilience, adaptability and flexibility are often also the times when we're experiencing uncomfortable emotions. The healthier our relationship is with our uncomfortable emotions, the greater our chance of smoothly and successfully navigating turbulent or uncharted waters.

8. THE SOCIAL DIMENSION

Take responsibility and converse for connection in service

'It may be true that morality cannot be legislated, but behaviour can be regulated. It may be true that the law cannot change the heart, but it can restrain the heartless.'
—Dr Martin Luther King

A German couple arrived at the airport hotel lobby one evening after their flight to New Zealand had been cancelled. They'd been directed by their airline to this hotel and promised a bed for the night. Standing beside them, I overheard the front-desk manager explain that there was 'no room at the inn' – they were fully booked despite the airline's promise. I could hear their hope fade and their fear rise as they looked at each other and spoke words of concern and disappointment in German.

The manager at the front desk saw it too, and asked them to wait. After a little while, he returned to explain that he'd made some phone calls to nearby hotels and had found one with a room available. He did this not because it would make the hotel money (it wouldn't) but because it was the right thing to do to be a good human. Sometimes, in service, it's not our problem to solve, but we solve it anyway.

One of the habits ServiceQ teaches early on in a Service Habits learning journey is to 'create helpful beliefs'. When service professionals carry a belief into their workplace that 'it's not my problem to solve this' or 'it's not my job to fix that', it can get in the way of looking after one another. In many situations, being helpful is just in the spirit of service.

Unconsciously, what the front-desk manager was doing in his encounter with the German couple was meeting their hard-wired need to feel that they were part of the 'tribe' and that the tribe wouldn't let them down. Humans need to feel we belong; we have always needed to band together to survive. So, the social dimension of service is an expression of our workplaces and communities, of our inherently social nature, to take care of one another as a species.

The contrast to feeling part of a tribe is feeling isolated and perhaps even invisible.

- Have you ever arrived at a party alone and waited for someone to make you feel welcome and bring you into the group? How long before you start to feel awkward, embarrassed or even sad?
- Have you ever arrived at your first day of work in a new place and waited for someone to welcome you and make you feel part of the team?
- Have you ever walked into a retail store and been completely ignored the whole time you're browsing?

Feeling invisible taps into the primitive feeling of being excluded from our tribe. It's not rational how bad it feels. The experience of being invisible or ignored is worse than you'd think because of our nature as tribal animals.

Over the past few years, the remote working movement has highlighted the impact of working in isolation. Without the social interaction and support of colleagues, remote workers report feeling cut off from their team and company culture, leading to feelings of disengagement and reduced productivity.

Employee isolation can also negatively affect mental health, particularly for those who live alone or don't have a good support network outside of work. Without the ability to socialise and interact in person with colleagues, remote workers may experience feelings of loneliness and depression, which can impact their overall wellbeing and job performance.

There is a strong argument that remote work increases productivity by reducing commuting time and costs, improving work-life balance and offering greater employee autonomy. However, remote working arrangements must be implemented thoughtfully and with the right infrastructure and support.

Remote work and working from home have positive and negative impacts on our social interaction skills, too. On the one hand, we can stay connected with colleagues and friends through digital communication tools such as email, videoconferencing and instant messaging. We can collaborate and socialise even when we're physically apart.

On the other hand, the lack of in-person and face-to-face communication means that nonverbal communication – body language, tone of voice and facial expressions – is reduced or lost altogether. This can make it harder to accurately interpret the intentions and emotions of others and can lead to miscommunications and misunderstandings.

If you think about the previous three chapters, the workplace is a crucial environment for gaining experience and strengthening the physical, cognitive and emotional dimensions of being human.

The lack of social interaction has contributed significantly to the deterioration of service standards – people have simply forgotten what it's like to be around others. Keeping humans involved in the critical touchpoints of the service chain and customer journey keeps people connected. In the future, if we're even more reliant on technology for communication and collaboration, with ever fewer opportunities for face-to-face interactions, this may stunt our social skills development.

Part of delivering great service is remembering that each person you interact with, regardless of who they are and their background, needs to feel a connection.

Service from humans strengthens our moral compass

We are all cousins. I feel this most when I travel to Greece with my partner. I can't speak Greek; I am not Greek, yet the moment I'm in the presence of the Greeks, I feel like I am Greek. A switch in my mind tells me that while I'm here, I should try to be more like them, eat, speak, laugh, and live like them. It's not that I want to be someone I'm not; I'm demonstrating respect for their culture, way of living and behaving – following a universal moral code of respect, friendliness and kindness. The pay off for me is I feel I belong.

And it's in the ordinary, small interactions while I am visiting Greece (or any place for that matter) that this moral compass is reinforced. Regardless of where you were raised or what country you came from, shared values and ways of treating people reinforce that there is no 'them'; it's all 'us'. This is what creates a social bond that has the potential to make us feel connected to the locals, even when we're not local.

But our moral compass is fragile, and we are, too. As much as the digital era is giving us technology for good purposes, the part that feels a bit like a force for evil is how it so easily and stealthily separates us from each other. Consequently, we're at risk of losing the practice of communicating differently, experiencing different world views and cultures and seeing the power of a universal moral code that brings people together.

> *'Ethics is how we behave when*
> *we decide we belong together.'*
> —David Steindl-Rast

The global responses to COVID-19 exposed the failures of communities. Being isolated led to a lack of social cohesion. Morals and ethical frameworks were tested, along with democratic values. Access to healthcare was poor; remote work and education tested families, and the slow economic recovery led to feelings of fear and anxiety.

A significant disruption to community cohesion and resilience highlights the need for shared ethics and democratic principles. Having said that, we don't need a significant crisis to chip away at society's moral compass. Each day, simple innovations are at risk of driving more of a wedge between fellow humans. Take the mundane activity of going to a supermarket. The push to transform super-markets with speedier checkout lanes and self-serving options is possibly overshadowing the fact that a local supermarket, for some people, is their community.

In 2019, a Dutch supermarket introduced slow checkouts for lonely elderly people who want someone to talk to. The move proved so successful that they installed the checkouts in 200 stores and added a 'chat corner' where locals could meet and have a coffee. My father, who is in his late 70s, lives on his own and quite likes it that way. But he, too, is consciously aware of the human interactions in his local town that make him happy. He chooses to go to the super-market every second day to interact with people, see familiar faces and be recognised by them.

Service interactions, as ordinary and repetitive as they may seem, are the most accessible place to make changes regarding ethics and strengthening our tribes. More customer journeys in all industries and businesses must incorporate human-to-human connections to maintain harmony and togetherness in society.

We need to serve the future. We must recognise that our actions today, as small as they may be, will greatly impact future generations.

There comes a time when the interest of people is more import-ant than the interest of profits. It feels like, more often than not, society falls under some kind of spell. People have become addicted to short-term thinking driven by profits and instant gratification and have lost sight of the long-term collective vision for how we treat each other.

When we see that our purpose and role is to serve strangers, it helps reinforce to people that we have a stake in others. There is an interconnectedness and mutual responsibility in service that aligns with our interdependence for the rest of life.

Something I have innately understood about service but not had the language to describe until these past few years is this: service directly reflects how well we survive as a social species. Being together and mindful of our social interactions is in our biology, and our social relationships are essential to our health and happiness as a community. Look around. If a bunch of aliens were to land on your patch of dirt right now and observe how we serve one another. What conclusions would they make about us as a species and our ability to survive even the most challenging times?

None of us needs a political career to be an influencer on social media or to have a YouTube following of 100,000 subscribers to take responsibility for the health of our community. Wherever you are and whatever you're doing right now, you contribute to the shared humanity of our time and future generations. And service is one of the easiest places to influence others.

> 'Not all of us can do great things,
> but we can do small things with great love.'
> —Mother Teresa

So, where do you start to strengthen social cohesion and social intelligence? It seems like such a big concept. Following are three simple techniques for you to practise. Imagine if every person in your organisation took responsibility and used these techniques. How much the connection in service to each other would be enhanced!

A snapshot of how to embody the social dimension

POINTS OF FAILURE	KEYS TO OVERCOMING	EXAMPLE TECHNIQUE
Ignore someone or diminish their importance	Recognise and validate individuals	Acknowledge people immediately
Service ethics disappear	Bring people together	Look for shared values
Change who you are and try to fit in	Be courageous and share your authentic self	Facilitate real conversations

Technique 1: Acknowledge people immediately

At ServiceQ, we recommend that frontline staff acknowledge people within a time or a spatial frame, like 5 seconds or 2 metres. Most people believe you're doing well if you greet customers within 30 seconds of arrival, but let's test this. Picture entering a retail store. Now check your watch or set your phone stopwatch and count 30 seconds. You'll likely realise that 30 seconds feels like a long time, so the goal is to acknowledge customers within 5 seconds. Similar to the 5-second time frame, the 2-metre spatial frame is a trigger for acknowledging people when they come within 2 metres of your space.

Acknowledging someone doesn't necessarily mean you have to serve them. But a simple nod, a smile with eye contact, or just saying, 'I'll be with you in a few minutes' all work a treat, even when you're busy.

Mr Willie, an older gentleman who works in Walmart, has one job: to greet people when they come through the store's doors. That's it. How he does it is quirky and memorable, and it's definitely within 5 seconds. He gives each person a closed fist bump gesture, like you would when you give a high five to someone and simultaneously shouts, 'Bam!' Watch the YouTube video for yourself (https://www.youtube.com/watch?v=qPMOYLA0KTo). It's quite cool and a wonderful example of one person taking the greeting to a new level in a timely, high-impact kind of way.

Technique 2: Look for shared values

We're not machines full of selfish genes who are always scheming to outdo each other, only ever showing kindness if there's some benefit to ourselves. We often achieve the greatest success in business and life when generously focused on others. We're all in this together; we raise each other up. Recognising what's good for the community puts you in service to humanity and is usually good for you, too.

The most fabulous documentary series, *Chimp Empire*, follows families and tribes of chimpanzees in the Ngogo rainforest, showing how they live and cooperate in their communities. Chimpanzees are incredibly emotional and political about who leads the hunt and the way they hunt, who they groom and the way they groom. After watching the series, I learned how much more complex they are than I'd realised; many of their behaviours are driven by hierarchy, political powers and the agenda of the alpha male. As much as humans are wired differently from chimpanzees, we do have a common need for rules of engagement to bring harmony to the tribe. When our moral compass is unclear, our rules of engagement are blurred, and it's difficult to bring people together and create team alignment.

The data that I've collected over the last 10 years in my business, ServiceQ, is that people working in all different sized companies crave a clear set of values and core behaviours that they can relate to and identify with as a group – often described as, 'It's the way we do things around here!'

Values, whether conscious or unconscious, are the motivation for every decision made or action taken. This is why we like to get people to become aware of their values, team values and, ultimately, service values. When we're clear about our values, we can clearly define the desired behaviours and actions we wish to see from each person. And with shared values, we can achieve shared accountability.

When you first walked into your workplace, you brought a set of values. These values are then influenced every day by the values you experience at work. When you're choosing where to work, what you value is closely related to what will make you stay and what will make you leave.

To be an integral part of a team, business and community is to be recognised as someone others can depend on, someone who has the values and behaviours of the tribe. Service starts with values and behaviours. Get clarity on those and you are one step closer to an alignment in your service team.

Technique 3: Facilitate real conversations

Have you ever had a decent conversation in a lift? It's a weird social experiment, in a way: you stand in a small metal box with a bunch of strangers, and you often, within a matter of seconds, feel unspoken social pressure descend on you to say something, anything . . . unless of course you have your face buried in a mobile device or headphones on.

Often, a lift or a lobby area is where you can witness some small talk, which can feel uncomfortable, pointless and even boring for some people. However, small talk in service starts a connection, creating some rapport before you get down to business, solving the problem or helping the customer.

Small talk doesn't have to be awkward or shallow, either. You can find value in small talk by making it interesting for both you and the other person; perhaps the small talk will eventually evolve into a more meaningful conversation. Small talk is a good beginning but far from enough to create a connection and learn more about the other person.

In service, one of the goals is to learn new information about the other person, the customer. To achieve this, quickly facilitating real conversations, even within moments, is a crucial skill. To practise the art of facilitating real conversations, think of your 'service small talk' as being like casting a fishing net out in a specific area of a lake. You'll get a bite in some areas and nothing in others, but you have to throw the net to try.

So, once you ask a broad question to a customer such as, 'How has your day been so far today?' or 'What else have you got planned after this?', you can use the bite from that lateral question and then ask a more specific vertical question. When you ask a vertical question, you then have a deeper conversation. Here are two examples.

Example 1

You: 'Thank you for your call. How has your day been so far today?'

Customer: 'Well, it's been okay; just got back from walking my dog in the park.'

You: 'That's nice! I'm a dog lover, too. What kind of dog do you have?'

Example 2

You: 'What else have you got planned after this?'

Customer: 'I am going to take my kids to a local amusement park.'

You: 'Oh, that sounds like great fun! I took my family to one last summer. Which park are you going to?'

A vertical question is a follow-up question once you've cast the net wide with your first lateral question. This helps foster a deeper connection by showing interest in the customer as a human and makes them feel that you've treated them more personally. Deep connections can be fast; you just need to keep things real.

9. THE SPIRITUAL DIMENSION

Purposefully and unexpectantly fulfil a need for meaningful service

'Our purpose transforms to serving whatever is needed, not what we predefined as purposeful. We open to the world that is, curious to discover what is needed from us, willing to engage on the world's terms, not ours.'

—Margaret J Wheatley

I was sitting in a work conference with 28 other humans when the facilitator asked us all a question and said we had half an hour to discuss and answer it. The question was, 'What's the meaning of work?'

Once we started hearing people's contributions, it was clear that this roomful of humans believed that work had far more meaning than money and employee benefits. They said things like this:

- 'Work complements my life and gives me order.'
- 'Work brings me closer to people and gives me connection.'
- 'Work allows me to contribute to others and make an impact.'
- 'Work inspires me to be better and do things I wouldn't do alone.'

The word 'work' is associated with different things by different people; perhaps with a sacrifice, some form of effort, or an identity that they hold on to, their contribution to the world, the effort for something they want further down the track, or for the service of good and of others. The clearer we are about our relationship to work, the easier showing up for work can be on the more challenging days.

Service in the spiritual dimension is what keeps us connected as humans. For this reason, I genuinely believe service is one of the most crucial ways to heal and help humanity. When we lack the spiritual dimension in meetings, team training sessions, our families and communities, and our daily service exchanges – that's what separates us from each other and life.

Three years ago, I never would have included the word 'spiritual' in a book, let alone dedicate a whole dimension and, therefore, chapter to it. But I sense and observe that many people who, over the years, have denied that we are spiritual beings having a human experience are now more open to making sense of what this means. Perhaps they're even ready to fully embody what this looks like.

This book intended to shine a light on and provide a road map for the future of service. If we don't bring the human spirit into this blueprint, we choose a path that looks no different to the past. And we'd be at risk of missing out on the richness of what it really means to feel fulfilled and to fulfil the needs of others.

We've known that fulfilling needs is important for centuries. I always think about the quote from American philosopher John Dewey, *The deepest urge in human nature is the desire to be important*'. If you dig a little deeper into Dewey and his philosophy of human nature, he explains that humans, as a highly developed state in the evolutionary process, are complex because of our ability to develop meaning in our actions. And service is one of those actions at work that can carry a lot of meaning for people.

With a saturation of consumerism and materialism on this planet, many have been led to believe that 'to be important' means 'to be liked', 'to be successful' or 'to be powerful'. In fact, all Dewey was saying was that 'to be important' is about being meaningful to someone or something.

The spiritual dimension is the pinnacle. It's the difference between good and great. It makes an exchange unique and memorable and is the quickest way to build loyalty with another person.

People lose their way when they lose their 'why'

At a recent awards night, a client of ServiceQ put on quite the celebration to recognise airport employees who had stood out from the crowd over the year. The room was full of corporate colleagues dressed up in bling ball gowns and penguin suits to celebrate the service excellence seen among them. The recipient of the humanitarian award was given to a lady by the name of Jackie, a cleaner. Jackie had come from a developing country, and English wasn't her first language. She was recognised for her human spirit and small daily acts of kindness at work. Her speech left no dry eye in the ballroom as she spoke from her heart about what it means to be a cleaner at an airport.

Jackie's 'why' was clear; she knew her purpose at work and saw that scrubbing toilets and changing bins was an opportunity to make someone's day. Each time she encountered someone, Jackie saw it as an opportunity to show her human spirit. Your 'why' doesn't need to be any more than this. It just needs to be bigger than you.

I recently read a post on social media about a man named Dale Schroeder who grew up in poverty, never married and had no children. He worked as a carpenter at the same company for 67 years and only owned two pairs of jeans. He spent his life savings sending 33 strangers to college. His 'why' was about giving people who wanted to be educated that opportunity, using money he didn't need himself.

Your 'why' doesn't need to be for personal gain; it needs to fulfil you. When we lose our 'why', life can feel a little lacking – less fulfilling – and leave us a little lost. When we are clear on what lights us up and taps into the part of our human spirit that makes us feel good, we find it much easier to stick with life's mundane and menial tasks.

The spiritual dimension relates to our inner growth and is incredibly character-building. When you find ways to let go of your self-focus and be more others-focused, and when you can activate something within the person you are serving, you ultimately create a meaningful exchange with them. The selfless action for the wellbeing of others, without expectation of reward or recognition, is at the core of exceptional service.

The hidden gem of service excellence: knowing the customer's 'why'

Our greatest goal in service is to meet and exceed the expectations of the person we're serving. But how well are people reading the expectations of others? You can see that the spiritual dimension extends all previous dimensions. For example, reading customers' emotions more accurately (the Emotional dimension) is foundational to reading their expectations.

How complicated have we made it in our minds, processes and marketing attempts to exceed these expectations, to give the unexpected, without realising that perhaps the best way to exceed the expectation of someone else is to tap into what they give meaning to, what their motivations are and their 'why'?

A popular business adage says, 'No one wants a drill. What they want is a hole. People don't want quarter-inch drill bits. They want quarter-inch holes'. In other words, what is the deeper need for your customer beyond their initial want? Why do they need a hole? What will the hole do for the person who wants it? In other words, be clear on the benefit of the hole, not the drill and the quarter-inch drill bits. This selling tactic is a clever way of talking about the deeper meaning of a product.

In every ordinary interaction of service, a deeper need, a more unconscious need, lies beneath the surface. The spiritual dimension taps into that.

- A busy working mum with three kids goes to get her car washed. Beyond the desire for a clean and tidy car, the unconscious need might be *taking time to take care of herself.*
- An elderly man walks into a high-street retail store. Beyond his desire to buy a new shirt, the unconscious need might be to *feel he is still modern despite his age.*
- A software engineer hosts a meeting to brief another department on a new update. Beyond his desire to meet his professional

responsibilities, the unconscious need might be to *feel he is seen and respected by colleagues he has never met.*

Those who serve best uncover these hidden unconscious needs and can serve from this place.

- The employee who takes the working mum's money at the end of the car wash shows the lady a number to call to pre-book next time, saying, *'You must be busy taking care of your children. Here's a way to make it a little bit easier to take care of yourself'.*
- The shop assistant who helps the elderly man with his shirt selection sees similarities between the customer and her father. She says, *'You have a similar build to my father; he always looks great in these shirts. I'd recommend this shirt to him if he were here today'.*
- The colleague in the meeting room approaches the software engineer at the end of the meeting and says, *'Thank you for making this tech talk easy to understand. I appreciate the way you translated this for us'.*

The future of service requires people to see what hidden meaning lies underneath the surface of an ordinary service exchange.

The spiritual dimension sits at the top of the pyramid because a life without relationships, where we focus purely on accomplishing things for ourselves, is unfulfilling and meaningless. People who serve from the spiritual dimension can tap into something we can do daily when available, consciously willing to stay present and prepared to dig below the surface.

It's like being a jeweller with a unique lens that reveals the hidden facets in a seemingly ordinary stone. (I am drawn to stones, crystals and rocks, so this metaphor makes sense to me.) The stone might appear dull, mundane and commonplace to the untrained eye. But to the jeweller, every curve, cut and angle tells a story. They can perceive the hidden colours, appreciate the microscopic inclusions, and recognise the potential for transformation within the rough stone.

Similarly, if someone whose role it is to serve another person can derive deeper meaning from ordinary exchanges – if they can spot the hidden emotions, interpret the unspoken words and uncover the subtle nuances that many may miss – they are entering a relationship with that person and, therefore, tapping into the spiritual dimension. This keen perception and understanding enables them to create precious connections from ordinary interactions, much like the jeweller crafting a beautiful gemstone from what looks like a rough rock.

Let me share three simple techniques for achieving a deeper understanding and applying the spiritual dimension. Again, no matter what your industry, job role or perspective in your workplace is, these techniques apply to you – and to anyone who seeks fulfilment in life.

A snapshot of how to embody the spiritual dimension

POINTS OF FAILURE	KEYS TO OVERCOMING	EXAMPLE TECHNIQUE
Going through the motions	Work with purpose and meaning	Know your 'why'
Self-focus	Commit to being other-focused	Choose to serve
Know-it-all	Search for truth	Seek wisdom in stillness

Technique 1: Know your 'why'

When you get clear as to why you do something, the clarity then helps drive your performance. Beyond performance, it provides that sense of purpose and meaning that we all yearn for in our ordinary days.

> *'May you live long enough to know*
> *why you were born.'*
> —Cherokee birth blessing

One person's 'why' may be to serve fabulous meals each day to make people feel at home. Another person's 'why' may be to fix cars to make people feel safe and independent. Everyone's 'why' will be different, and that is perfect. Where you are in life, your family, your finances, your living circumstances, your sense of self, your growth and development, your goals and your ambitions – these are just some of the reasons your why will be personal and unique. You don't need to compare your why to anyone else's – if you can see it brings you energy and passion each day to do what you do, that's enough. What we all have in common, however, is that we all desire a 'why'.

If you're to be a fully expressed 5-dimensional human being at work and create meaningful exchanges with the people you serve, the first place to tap into meaning is yourself. Reflection questions are a great way to start clarifying what your work means to you and, more broadly, what your 'why' is. For example:

- What's the meaning of work for me?
- What makes me want to get out of bed each day and go to work?
- What parts of my work make me most happy and energised?

Technique 2: Choose to serve

The best way to serve is not necessarily your skill but rather your decision to commit to serve.

This technique is the first Service Habit I unpacked in my book *Service Habits* (2nd ed.). When the team at ServiceQ facilitates learning this habit, it's presented as a mindset technique to help people get in the zone and remember that other people experience us from moment to moment. To upgrade this Service Habit, we need to look at this technique in the context of the spiritual dimension.

When you commit to the outcome of serving someone, you are sharply focused on them. Being other-focused allows you to experience more meaningful experiences with the other person because you aren't distracted by alternative decisions. Indecision, by contrast, would keep you shallow, and your attention and focus would be thinly spread. The choice to be 'all-in' on service, at that moment, leaves the other person feeling a greater connection to you. You will also feel a greater connection to yourself.

From a philosophical point of view, life is meaningless to you if you decide that your choices have no meaning. From a very practical point of view, choosing to serve each day requires you to let go of being completely self-focused and dig into a part of yourself that is genuinely available and willing to help someone or something bigger than you.

> *'Virtue means doing the right thing, in relation to the*
> *right person, at the right time, to the right extent,*
> *in the right manner, and for the right purpose.'*
> —Aristotle

Sometimes, service doesn't look like you had planned. Sometimes, service needs less of your brilliant ideas and clever solutions and more of your animal instinct and connection to a higher purpose. Sometimes, service invites you to loosen the grip of control and be okay with learning while serving.

When we see serving others as a way to learn more about ourselves and the people around us, service becomes a training ground for breeding spiritual virtues: kindness, humility, compassion, generosity, mercy, trustworthiness, sincerity, tenderness, patience, wisdom and love. These virtues are universal, and humans are drawn to them. That's why this 'technique' of choosing to serve will never fail you.

We all have these virtues, which are the tools for bringing meaning to our conversations and actions. We had them when we were born; we learn over time to use them, and then we learn over time to forget them. Humanity is at its very best when we're living with these attributes. And service is the place to bring them. At work, at home, at school, on the streets, with a stranger, with a customer . . . everywhere and anyone.

At this time in history, we are being asked to make it less about us and more about others. Less divided and more unified. When we do this, we find a greater connection back to self, and our spiritual growth accelerates. Connection with others can only be as deep as our connection to self.

What's your definition of 'Choose to serve'?

1. Think back to the time you accepted your current job role. Why did you choose to be a service professional in this role? What meaning do you give to your job role?

2. Recall moments when you've been in service to a family member or friend. What is it that you gain?

3. How is this part of your identity, and what character-building attributes were experienced by people on the receiving end of your service?

Technique 3: Seek wisdom in stillness

It's been said by many great teachers and mentors of our time that wisdom is the true nature of reality. Another way of thinking about this is to be open-minded and search for truth – in a service context, the other person's desires or needs. What will help you create a meaningful moment with someone in a service interaction?

I'll give you a clue as to what will not help you create meaningful moments: seeing the person you serve as simply a body and mind. Remember, each time someone is in front of you, they are made up of multiple layers, and each one of us is so deep, vast and magical that perhaps they are unaware of it. But you, because you are wise and still, can see in them what they maybe have forgotten about within themselves.

Park your cleverness, be intellectually humble and recognise that what makes you most brilliant at service is seeing the other person's reality – what's really going on for them.

Wisdom is the sense of the big picture. The ability to rise above the thought traps, biases, and preconceived ideas of what you think is needed. To have the brilliance and courage to dig deeper and search beyond the seen.

When you see and explore the potential meaning of an ordinary interaction – as with the mother at the car wash, the elderly man at the retail store and the software engineer in the meeting room – you are speaking to their heart, possibly even their soul.

A wonderful place to start here is to practise this sequence when you have the honour of serving someone else:

1. Slow down.
2. Become still.
3. Ask questions.

So, now we've come to the end of the 5D chapters, it's time to bring your attention back to how to lead this, now and into the future.

Part 3

LEADING THE CHARGE

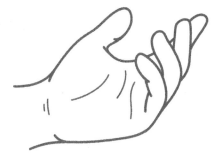

10. GAME-CHANGERS

Leading the 5D Revolution

We watch you when you arrive; you set the tone the moment you speak.
We seek your input and advice; you make decisions each hour, day and week.
We make it tricky for you, occasionally, because of our different personalities.
We serve the customers the way you serve us.
We feel the value we bring when you praise us.
It's a job that isn't everyone's cup of tea, and yet so many of you
are thrown into it with no leadership maturity.
The best of you leaves the biggest imprint, by making our jobs in
service much easier to win.

If you've turned to this page after reading the chapters before it, I want to say, 'You're probably already doing a great job'. To be curious, open and willing to learn more each day is a wonderful trait in a leader and sets up a strong foundation for leading into the future.

Right now, there is a quiet, urgent, undeniable need for leaders to aspire to and restore humanity in business. We need a revolution in workplaces and how people serve each other. Will you go on this odyssey of growth?

When you're faced with life-changing challenges, you need to act. However, you can't achieve success and results in business single-handedly: the better your people are, the better the business will be. So, the ultimate question you must ask to lead the 5D Revolution is this: *'Do those I serve grow?'* Are they happier, wiser, healthier, better off from working with you and in your business? Are they creating ripples that positively impact the people around them?

If you can, think back to a time when you felt the engagement and connection of your teams and witnessed the value they placed on how they contributed at work. At that time, you were leading from a place that was less about 'me' and more about 'we', and that's what's necessary now. Not only will your staff and your organisation benefit, but so will the community.

Leadership is hard, and it's even harder now than it was in the past. The erosion of service in society reflects the decline of our humanity – our changed world now encourages people to focus on their self-interest.

The wealthy protect their wealth.

The leaders protect their power.

The people protect their comfort.

These are some of the reasons why certain workplace cultures lack resilience. Seeking superficial gains in profits and short-term pleasures and lacking deeper values eventually catches up with an organisation. It erodes trust and the human spirit that believes in treating others with dignity and respect. We are seeing evidence of this worldwide.

Big tech companies such as Google, Meta and Apple have been criticised for how they manage user privacy and data handling, creating mistrust.

In the United States, pharmaceutical company Purdue Pharma

has been critiqued for its aggressive marketing tactics and for downplaying the addiction risk of its opioid OxyContin, leading to significant harm to customers.

American financial institution Wells Fargo has been exposed: its employees created over a million unauthorised bank accounts to meet their sales targets. This greed has led to significant reputational damage.

Were the leaders of these organisations doing it for themselves or for others?

Imagine the change that could occur, despite the present-day instability, fear and unrest, if leaders of organisations and communities acted for the sake of others. Just like a host holding the door for you at a café, a great leader would ensure everyone got through before they did – leading for the sake of others and creating conditions that help people tap into their full potential. The leaders help others protect their peace.

Just imagine what it would be like to drive into your workplace and see engaged employees and happy customers – consistently.

In the digital age, leaders need to focus on others. This is the future of service.

If I were to define leadership for the future and what it means to lead the 5D Service Revolution, I would say this: ***it's about creating the conditions so everyone's skills shine and getting the stuff done that matters to others.***

> *'Life's most persistent and urgent question is,*
> *"What are you doing for others?"'*
> —Dr Martin Luther King

Game-changing 5D Service leadership

I have to constantly remind myself that what I was taught in the past – how I was taught to lead – is not what the future will reward. I think back to some of the ways I used to lead a team in my 20s and 30s, and it's just so far from who I am today and what I understand about influencing and creating trust so that people want to follow me. It's not that past leadership styles were wrong or broken; it's just that the world was less messed up than it is now, and humanity was not as evolved as it is today. What I'm saying is that what worked for us back then was perfect at the time, but it won't work for us now. We've evolved and leadership needs to evolve with us.

It's time to break with what we have understood 'leading people' involves and imagine a game-changing new leadership style: 5D Service leadership.

Leadership in today's world can feel uncertain and even a little mysterious. Sometimes, it feels like leaders who have some sort of magic touch with people and simultaneously get the results for the business must have superpowers. We are magnificent and incredibly influential on the people around us. Your potential is limitless, which is also true for the people – your teams – who follow you as their leader. One of the most magnificent superpowers a leader has is to see and hold belief in people long before they believe in themselves. You can literally change the weather of your organisation's culture and how people treat each other just by how you lead.

Some leaders adopt a self-serving leadership style, and it is like a thunderstorm, fierce and destructive, where the leader's actions only serve to fuel their own ego, leaving chaos in their wake. In contrast, some leaders adopt a 5D Service leadership style that is like a gentle rain, nurturing and refreshing, as the leader's actions shower support and care upon their team, helping them grow and flourish. Both get the job done, but with different lasting results.

Whenever humans are involved, the ego is always present. For this reason, it's essential to continually ask yourself, 'Am I doing this for the sake of others or to further my own interests?' When the ego is present and ruling the show, that's self-serving leadership. When the ego is present but is not ruling the show, that's service leadership. It's up to you to check in and see whether your ego is ruling.

Below is a simple contrast between self-serving leadership and 5D Service leadership.

Self-serving leadership	5D Service leadership
Control-orientated Self-serving leaders tend to exercise a high degree of control over their teams and the work being done, often micromanaging tasks and making decisions unilaterally.	**Empowerment** 5D Service leaders aim to empower their team members, fostering an environment where individuals feel confident and capable of taking initiative.
Lack of empathy Self-serving leaders lack empathy, showing little understanding or consideration for the feelings and needs of their team members.	**Empathy** 5D Service leaders show understanding and consideration for the feelings and needs of their team members, promoting a supportive work environment.
Self-promotion Self-serving leaders often prioritise their own success and recognition over that of their team members or the overall organisation.	**Collaboration** 5D Service leaders value teamwork and encourage collaborative problem-solving and decision-making processes.
Short-term focus Self-serving leaders may focus on achieving short-term goals, sometimes at the expense of long-term sustainability and growth.	**Long-term vision** 5D Service leaders focus on long-term goals and sustainability, prioritising these over short-term gains.

Self-serving leadership	5D Service leadership
Resistance to feedback Self-serving leaders may not take kindly to criticism or suggestions, viewing them as threats rather than opportunities for growth or improvement.	**Openness to feedback** 5D Service leaders are receptive to feedback and see it as a valuable tool for improvement and growth for themselves and their teams.
Neglect of employee development Self-serving leaders often don't invest in their employees' growth and development, viewing people as tools to achieve their own objectives rather than valuable assets with potential.	**Investment in people** 5D Service leaders invest in the growth and development of their team members, viewing them as valuable assets and recognising their potential.

Following is a summary of some beliefs that will be helpful when the ego is ruling and you want to lead with a 5D Service leadership approach.

The fundamental beliefs of a 5D Service leader

I believe that:	My job as a 5D Service leader is to:
caring for others has a ripple effect.	take care of my people so they will take care of others.
leadership doesn't mean you have all the answers.	unleash my people's potential by asking them questions.
motivation is temporary.	inspire behaviour change, not merely motivate.
people want to feel they belong.	create the conditions for connection through values.
people seek meaning in their work.	seek feedback and celebrate the wins that individuals and the team contribute to.

Your legacy

You never know what legacy you're leaving, but I can guarantee you are leaving one.

5D Service leadership enables you to weave a story of profound impact. You are already rising and evolving, and soon, I hope you'll embody the change that we need to see and wish to inspire in others. You can become the beacon of inspiration that will empower this customer service revolution far more than a customer service revolution. You can help create a safe haven for your people to nurture their wellbeing and enable them to transcend their limits.

However, it's possible that your desire to leave a legacy could be getting in the way of serving others. It's possible that focusing more on the answers is getting in the way of others finding their answers.

The invitation to lead the 5D Service Revolution is this:

- Leave your legacy: please do – one that's not for personal gain but rather a legacy of how you helped others achieve what they needed.
- Provide answers: please do – but focus less on what you know and be more curious about the unknown.
- Strive for results: hell yeah – and know that how you get the results is more important than the results themselves.

I've been incredibly inspired by the work of Margaret J Wheatley, who writes for leaders just like you and me. In her book *Who Do We Choose To Be?*, she speaks in a way that truly makes you sit up a little taller and want to be better. Here's one of my favourite excerpts from her book; it summarises your potential legacy:

> 'We need leaders who recognize the harm being done to
> people and planet through the dominant practices that
> control, ignore, abuse, and oppress the human spirit.
> We need leaders who put service over self, stand steadfast
> in crises and failures, and who display unshakable faith
> that people can be generous, creative, and kind.'
>
> (Wheatly, 2017)

11. THE 5D SERVICE LEADERSHIP FRAMEWORK

A practical guide for implementation

*'To plant a seed, watch it grow, to tend it and then harvest
it offered a simple but enduring satisfaction.
The sense of being the custodian of this small patch
of earth offered a small taste of freedom.*

*'In some ways, I saw the garden as a metaphor for certain
aspects of my life. A leader must also tend his garden;
he, too, sows seeds, and then watches, cultivates
and harvests the result.'*

—Nelson Mandela

Implementing 5D Service requires journeying on an uncharted path. Hold my hand. I've got you. We'll do this together and have some fun along the way.

Like you, I'm a custodian of service. Custodians must bring belief and confidence and provide a plan that supports people on their transformational journey. I'm about to share everything I know about implementing 5D Service into your world – the dos and don'ts of reimagining a new consciousness in customer service.

The framework in this chapter will set you up to take the leap from ordinary to extraordinary service interactions. It's a simple framework to follow and to lead from, with practical ways of implementing 5D Service, no matter the size of your business or the geographical spread of your people.

Having said that, you are the gardener of your own garden, and the plan I'm sharing with you is simply a way to fertilise and sprout growth in your 5D Service culture. Like a garden, be mindful that your interpretation of 5D Service will differ depending on your environment.

Warning: Tipping point ahead!

If you feel like your business has reached a tipping point – a critical juncture where a relatively minor change can produce a significant outcome – you can use this chapter to propel yourself into action. What have you got to lose? It may feel like your business is fragile and that undercurrents indicate a significant shift is on the horizon. Perhaps:

- standards have dropped and you need to raise the bar on what is expected of your people
- planned results are not being reached
- talent in the business is leaving, which is slowing down the innovation you need to stand out from your competitors
- shareholders have lost faith in you
- the market is changing, and you're at risk of becoming irrelevant
- customers are leaving and not returning.

It might feel like the moment before a row of dominoes begins to fall. They've been set up, nudged close together, and the slightest touch will create a chain reaction.

I want to suggest a different tipping point, one that you proactively set up to create positive change. To generate momentum towards a particular outcome that's unstoppable and irreversible. Rather than watch the dominoes fall, we'll watch the dominoes create a beautiful ripple effect through the space they occupy.

Be aware that once a system has tipped, it can't return to its former state. People need to learn to live with it, to adapt – for some, this isn't possible. In other words, there will most likely be casualties when you implement this plan. Some people will not embrace the 5D way, and that's okay. We love them anyway.

This is not about being liked or popular, or holding on to people in our teams who are not performing because we're afraid of difficult conversations. What it's about is putting the customer and the collective performance of the business at the centre of your decision-making and, therefore, your leadership approach.

Be mindful of the objections you will receive when implementing 5D Service. Most likely, you will hear a version of these three:

1. 'We don't **believe** this soft-stuff approach will get the results.'
   If this objection is raised, ask people to consider how this belief is helpful and whether they could reframe it to be more open-minded and accepting that performance requires both technical and relational skills.

2. 'We don't have **time** to focus on the people stuff.'

   If this objection is raised, ask people to consider the time they spend on poor performance in service that leads to a lack of customer loyalty and employee engagement and potential rework for various touchpoints on a service journey. Slowing down and taking time to develop skills will eventually accelerate results if it's applied, as suggested in this chapter.

3. 'We don't have the **capability** or **resources** to train and develop 5D Service.'

   If this objection is raised, then be willing to look at some of the low-hanging fruit and the resources that you do have to offer as a starting point. Use that time to consider outsourcing support for training in areas where you don't have the capability or capacity.

Based on your environment, there may be more objections than the three mentioned above. The main point for preparedness for any implementation of this work is to make sure you've considered potential objections and have some well-thought-out responses to them. Deal with them head-first and at the beginning of any transformation journey like this 5D Service one.

Points of failure

Let's spend a moment understanding failure before sharing the conditions for implementation success.

Your relationship to failure is essential to understand. Trust me, I've been getting really clear about this, as I aim to become world-class in my work. It's not easy, but no one said it would be.

My mate, four-time Olympian Dan Collins, is an Olympic medal winner and is brilliant at helping people develop a winning team and culture. You can check him out at https://dancollins.com.au.

From his point of view (a high-performing-mindset point of view), failure is not defeat. Inevitably, when we stretch ourselves, we will come up short. So, if 5D Service feels like a bit of a stretch to you – excellent. Trust the process, and when you fail at one of the key implementation areas, do better next time! The outcomes or results you chase in the world are often based on chance. You won't be able to excel, deliver extraordinary service or propel your business into a different stratosphere if failure is a problem for you.

Over the past decade, my team at ServiceQ have been rolling out culture transformation programs to help change people's behaviours at work. You'll see some key points of failure (DON'Ts) and points of success (DOs) that we've summarised over the years, relating to each of the conditions for 5D Service that we'll cover in the rest of this chapter. They're worth noting!

Now, let's get into it.

Create the conditions for 5D Service

If you create the conditions for 5D Service – conditions that help people remember their human qualities – you'll still get the results you need at work, and you'll simultaneously make the work meaningful and impactful for the people you serve. Trust the process and follow the dos and don'ts to implement 5D Service in your team, business and community.

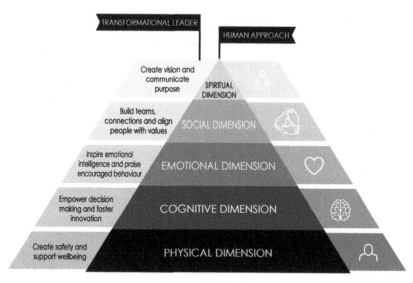

5D SERVICE

The physical dimension: Create safety and support wellbeing

The aim is to maintain a healthy culture by focusing on physical and psychological safety, and enable a culture of wellbeing to exist among doing the work.

Keeping people safe will help them rise to any challenge. Keeping them well will help them sustain rising to any challenge.

You want to fundamentally create psychological safety and physically safe environments to create trust. According to Amy Edmondson (Professor of Leadership and management at the Harvard Business School and best-selling author of *The Fearless Organization*), psychological safety is 'a belief that one will not be punished or humiliated for speaking up with ideas questions, concerns, or mistakes, and that the team is safe for interpersonal risk-taking' (Edmondson, 2018). One of my other favourite quotes from Edmondson is this:

> *'If you change the nature and quality of the conversations in your team, your outcomes will improve exponentially. Psychological safety is the core component to unlock this.'*
>
> (Edmondson, 2018)

Your teams reasonably expect their leaders to acknowledge and act on their concerns, or at least, they expect to have their concerns legitimately heard. This is the foundation of psychological safety. Of course, identifying these concerns is not enough; you must then act. Eradicating identified problems and proactively building a better workplace culture will create a more amicable, professional and psychologically safe workplace.

Companies that don't invest in their people, by contrast – that don't listen to them and have plans and processes for taking action when they raise concerns – often lose their most valuable staff members. Or worse, they keep their most toxic ones.

So, what's your job as a leader in creating psychological safety and wellbeing at work? A good analogy might be that of a fitness trainer. A good personal trainer helps their clients to exercise safely, increase their fitness and build their muscles. Clients will be uncomfortable during sessions, even feel stretched to their limits, but they will be safe. In the same way, your job as a leader is not to protect your team from discomfort. It's to protect them from harm and to help motivate them to push through discomfort to harness growth opportunities.

However, to support your people's wellbeing, you must first nail it for yourself. You're responsible for a lot of lives, so make sure you have a read on your own health. Just as your business's back-of-house areas promote a vibe for employees that translates to front-of-house with those they serve, the same is true of you! To lead with your best self means taking care of yourself so you can sustain your energy through tough times and increase your capacity to take care of others.

What exactly is wellbeing? According to a helpful *Psychology Today* article, wellbeing is 'the experience of health, happiness, and prosperity. It includes having good mental health, high life satisfaction, a sense of meaning and purpose, and the ability to manage stress. More generally, wellbeing is just feeling well' (Davis, 2019).

DON'T
- hide mistakes and blame others when there's been a service failure or a failure at a company-wide level
- roll out a wellbeing program to the business and ignore your own wellbeing
- leave back-of-house areas until last for upgrades and refurbishments.

DO
- create a safe environment for failure. Share the mistakes and what's been learned from failure, and invite everyone to openly share ideas and innovation in how to do better
- build routines on your best days to help you through your more challenging days
- take care of yourself and your own wellbeing
- invest in making your workplace an environment you would have happily welcomed the Queen into (god bless her soul).

The cognitive dimension: Empower decision-making and foster innovation

The aim is to empower teams to make better decisions and be more innovative in problem-solving in the moment.

In her book *Thinking in Bets*, Annie Duke beautifully articulated that decision-making is a lot like a game of poker. The real world, she explained, involves:

> 'uncertainty, risk, and occasional deception,
> prominent elements of poker. Poker . . . is a game
> of incomplete information. It is a game of
> decision-making under conditions of uncertainty
> over time . . . Valuable information remains hidden.
> There is also an element of luck in any outcome.
> You could make the best possible decision at every
> point and still lose the hand, because you don't know
> what new cards will be dealt and revealed.'
>
> (Duke, 2018)

Creating points of reference for your employees to empower their decision-making and foster innovation is fundamental to 5D Service. You need to teach your teams to play poker. Well, not really – but to think like poker players.

Know the rules

My book, *Service Habits* (2nd ed.), has a whole chapter dedicated to empowering your teams. It's called 'Bend blue rules'. The premise of the chapter is that you need to help teams apply common sense and good decision-making when an interaction requires new thinking, flexibility or bending an existing rule to suit the situation.

To do this, you need to distinguish between 'red rules' and 'blue rules'. Red rules are rules that cannot be broken. They involve decisions that could be detrimental to the organisation, such as a safety procedure or legal issue, such as serving alcohol to someone underage. Blue rules, by contrast, are designed to make the service or operation run more smoothly. They apply to decisions that can't harm the organisation – like an operational procedure or a refund policy – meaning they can be bent or broken if necessary.

Identifying the blue and red rules is one of the most empowering and proactive things a service team can do. By establishing what rules can be bent and giving people a framework for how to speak to the customer, they become more confident about dealing with 'grey area' issues in their leaders' absence. We still receive regular emails of thanks from one leader we've worked with, saying how empowering the 'blue rules/red rules' conversation was for their team.

Doing a 'blue rule or red rule' activity is a great way to exercise the brain. You and your team can practise using common sense and asking great questions that will solve problems in scenarios that are likely to occur or already occur. The goal is to give people permission to solve problems and provide a framework to help them identify problems and act confidently.

DON'T

- update processes or procedures that involve humans (employees or customers) without workshopping the scenarios first
- update rules without providing the 'why' behind the update for employees to connect with.

DO

- plan for future service scenarios, using personas and customer types to bring the simulation to life
- discuss the consequences of decisions that don't get the best outcome
- spend some time imagining where your business is heading and be willing to explore potential leadership-development needs or learning gaps for future success.

The emotional dimension: Inspire emotional intelligence and praise encouraged behaviour

The aim is to motivate teams to apply the desired behaviours and self-regulate their emotional responses at work.

5D Service leaders are monomaniacally focused on strengthening their teams' emotional intelligence (EI). If EI is still foreign in your business and is not intentionally taught, praised and measured, lean in and listen hard.

In the early 1990s, when science journalist Daniel Goleman wanted to publish a book on EI, he was told that emotions had no place in business and that companies were simply not supposed to care about that stuff. It wasn't until 1995 that his book *Emotional Intelligence* was published, popularising the framework presented in the ground-breaking 1990 paper also called 'Emotional Intelligence' by Peter Salovey and John Mayer. This paper contributed to a major shift in how organisations value EI, and it has become a widespread practice for companies to hire for it and teach it.

It's hard to believe that before that time, people found it difficult to fathom that 'emotions' lived on a spectrum of learning, where skills could be learned and strengthened. EI is a set of skills that help people accurately identify and express emotion in oneself and in others. When EI skills are applied effectively, you can regulate your own emotions and be better equipped to motivate others through theirs.

In the past, the focus in business was always on physical productivity – a calculation of manufacturing output and labour input. IQ was the standard of excellence. This is outdated now, and machines and computer algorithms embody the kind of logic that we humans used to be paid to use. They identify trends and patterns, learn from them, solve complex problems and calculate and share information to achieve particular outcomes. Our future focus needs to be EI: recognising how people feel and aiming to make them feel better.

You need your people to be less machine-like, to leave the algorithms to the computers and be more human-like, awakening our better human faculties.

Reward and recognise

A fabulous way to encourage the use of those stunning human faculties is to praise. One of the first questions I ask in any conversation with a new client is, 'What's your reward and recognition framework?' This immediately gives me some insights into the culture and how often people are recognised for their decision-making and creative ways of serving people.

When you scratch a little bit more, you can find out the criteria or why people are nominated for a reward or recognised in front of their peers – this demonstrates what contributions the company values. When people are recognised for their behaviours and how they managed a situation, it motivates and inspires others around them. It's much easier to explain a service interaction or a service moment that displayed EI and skill in a 'reward and recognition' conversation than it is to explain it in a training session.

A robust reward and recognition framework is crucial in a 5D Service culture. Set it up well. Clearly articulate the process and stick to it. When you praise well and praise often, you are motivating people by highlighting the progress of others and reinforcing what 'good work' looks like in action.

DON'T
- expect employees on a 5D Service transformation journey to change at the same pace as each other. We all start at different levels of skill in feeling, reading and balancing emotions
- strive for EI without 'good' behaviours being articulated and communicated
- ignore poor behaviour and poor capacity to self-regulate.

DO
- monitor and acknowledge all progress in individuals and be transparent about people grasping concepts at different speeds
- be explicit about the behaviours you wish to see in your teams
- recognise EI in feedback loops, both formal and informal
- reward and recognise people by sharing the story of their service and the impact their decisions and actions had on the other person.

The social dimension: Build teams and connections and align people with values

The aim is to inspire teams to connect and behave in ways aligned with the organisation's values.

Helping people feel connected to each other can be done intentionally but stealthily. Ideally, you want to be getting your people together often for various reasons; how you gather is the key to this area of implementation of 5D Service, and it requires an investment of time and money. Getting people together physically in a LIVE face-to-face environment will supercharge connection. Having said that, yes, online gatherings are super-useful when you have a geographic spread, and getting people together online is better than not gathering at all.

As for timing, don't wait for the perfect time to start investing in the social dimension of your 5D Service journey. If you think you have a burning platform, such as silos among teams, poor service scores, or a loss of customers or money, you'll benefit from getting your people together often. If you're performing well, with no real urgency or threat on the horizon for your service performance and business results – don't wait. Get going on building solid teams, no matter the climate. There's never any harm in bringing people together if there's a well-thought-out intention.

We saw this firsthand during the COVID-19 pandemic. One ServiceQ client, Melbourne Airport, dove right in and began a service transformation program across the entire airport community when they were still rebuilding their teams. The 'Stepping Forward' program was designed and delivered to do one thing: create extraordinary experiences for travellers no matter where they were in the airport. Twelve months after implementing the program's seven 'commitments' (behaviours), the airport won a Global Skytrax's award for Best Airport Staff in the Asia Pacific.

What I love about this example is that Melbourne Airport didn't wait for the crisis to end; they started a proactive transformation amid it. The leaders of this journey have been continually surprised at the level of engagement with and the results of the transformation program, especially the connection built across multiple organisations – including all the contractors and partners that comprise the 20,000-plus employees. No one is below or above the program; everyone is equal. The fundamental takeaway is that it has given people permission to step into the desired values regardless of their role; there's an expectation that people will know and act following the seven commitments.

5D Service and 5D Leadership are not about reacting to and fixing a problem; it's about ensuring your people and your business continually improve from a solid foundation to reach their full potential. Be extraordinary at service or run the risk of becoming irrelevant.

Team reflection

Team reflection is an integral component of the 5D Service Revolution. Once you have a set of shared behaviours and language, you must create the space to reflect on how well you're all living these values. Recently, the ServiceQ team had an offsite to revisit our own values and behaviours (which can be found on our website, www.serviceq.co/about-us). Creating values and behaviours is step one; however, if you take the conversation further, as we did at our team conference, you'll determine how to keep score of these behaviours.

Telling employees how you will measure them is expected in the business world. But to build greater accountability, high performance and a strong connection to your brand and the people in your teams, you, as the leader, are better off asking, 'What results do you want for each other?' instead. This question is far more empowering and elevating, and I guarantee it will stick. We mostly remember what we've co-created, not so much what we've been told to memorise – oh and then believe.

When I asked the ServiceQ team what results they wanted for each other, here's what they came up with.

Our Team Code at ServiceQ and how we keep score

Care
The 'I care more' score. Meaning 'I care more about my patch of the business than anyone else'.

Wellbeing
The 'I am in good shape' score. Meaning 'I take responsibility for my health and wellbeing, and I ask for help when I need it'.

Promise
The 'I keep my promise to the team' score. 'I am accountable for my words and actions, acknowledging their impact on the success of the whole team and the business.'

Performance
The 'I gave it my all' score. 'My character and my capability are the currency of my performance. We are all open to becoming better.'

Of course, team reflection can be done in various formats. However, I recommend scheduling quarterly offsites where your key talent can unplug and connect to some deeper thinking, have meaningful conversations and explore creative work with their colleagues. Take them offsite. Change up the environment and get them among nature.

For the past 10 years, I have had a ritual where I dedicate one full day every 90 days to work on the business and reflect. Spending this day among nature and in an environment that broadens my perspective always shows me something new, and the feeling of unplugging is palpable.

Create an advocacy group

The purpose of an advocacy group is for the members of the group to be the champions of the change you want. The group should comprise a diverse representation of employees at all levels of leadership and from various areas of the business. The more diverse the group, the better they'll perform.

An advocacy group is non-negotiable if you want to succeed in implementing 5D Service. Without one, you will soon find the transformation overwhelming and too hard.

The group must meet regularly. I like to set up a bi-monthly cadence for the first year; this can then drop back to one meeting a quarter. The meetings are better when they're facilitated by someone, and there's an agenda with lots of space for discussion and decision-making. Some of the questions the group will focus on are:

- Have we set the right priorities?
- Do we have the right resources?
- What is working well?
- What is not working well?

You want this group to feel fully empowered to set the direction of the transformation and oversee initiatives and things to stop doing. Their sole focus is on implementation.

DON'T
- settle on a vague set of values: they will be misinterpreted and hard to implement
- set and forget your values and behaviours with no measures or ways of seeing progress
- lead a transformation solo
- minimise the importance of having a team offsite.

DO
- describe explicit behaviours that are aligned with your values
- create relevant tools and measures to keep score of your teams' norms
- choose a team of champions (the advocacy team) to be the custodians of the transformation
- prioritise regular team offsites.

The spiritual dimension: Create a vision and communicate a purpose

The aim is to invite teams to see their work and efforts as contributing to something far greater than their self-interests.

The best way to communicate your visions and measure how well people live the company's purpose is to see what stories are being told. You need story stewardship!

Story stewardship

You must engage in story stewardship as part of your 5D Service transformation. When you nail your storytelling, like many great businesses do, you illuminate the collective meaning behind the business and articulate the people's contribution.

I always love it when a CEO in one of our ServiceQ training sessions shares a story about a service moment. When people listen to a story, you can see in people's faces that they're sharing the emotions of the people in the story, resulting in everyone feeling connected. Stories allow us to feel fully human and offer us meaning. They can help us connect to our past and improve our present.

When stories circulate in an organisation – whether via email, in a written letter, on a storyboard displayed somewhere, in a regular company newsletter or during a storytelling moment at a team gathering – regardless of the method, they create positive change and stretch people to do better. Stories have more critical information for people to learn from than any dry data or analytics can provide.

The best stories to communicate your vision and purpose are about the transformation or change your product or service made to the customer or other person.

Stories can help people see themselves in others. They can help people make sense of something, connect them to a greater purpose or desire, and help them see their potential, possibilities and unconscious needs. Stories allow us to express truths compassionately and kindly. They inspire people to lean in further and want more from the experience of working in your organisation. Look for stories. Gather and share them.

Making a strong start

If you're already sold and want to embark on the 5D Service journey, I recommend marking the occasion – drawing a line in the sand. When there's no clear line between the current state and the desired future state, it's difficult for people to envision the leap you're asking them to take. So, mark the occasion to make a strong start. Have a kick-off event. A moment to remember. Make it fun and engaging, and if you have to inspire people with treats or music, do that, too. This must be a sacred time when you show your team your commitment to this new way forward.

Then what?

Be in the room

I have countless examples and evidence to support the theory that if you want a service transformation or an uplift from where you are to where you want to take your team, it has to come from the top. The first requirement for the success of any service transformation is advocacy, belief and commitment from the leaders – from the top-dog CEO, GM or whoever runs the show through to the front-line leaders.

This is not about 'being interested' in a company-wide service program or doing the obligatory 'show face' at important meetings. Rather, it's about conveying the true message that 'I'm all-in on this journey with you, and conversations about the way we serve and develop skills for better behaviours in service are not beneath any of us'. A CEO serving his business community in this incredibly humbling and committed way profoundly impacts the desired transformation.

As a leader, it's not what you say that people remember; it's that you choose to be there, stay and participate till the end. Having leaders take part in a service transformation journey – whether a specific leadership pathway designed just for them or a journey for their broader team – has a 10x return on investment. You can expect to see:

- improved retention of employees
- happier customers
- healthier sales and profits.

So, be in the room.

DON'T
- show graphs of progress and change in your service
- kick off your training or transformation journey with an email
- come for the start of a conversation or training session then leave or lurk in the back of the room and watch what people say.

DO
- share stories that matter and connect people to meaning
- kick off your training and transformation journey with a cool event
- stay till the end of anything you're asking your people to attend and be with them, participating fully.

---

12. WHERE TO NOW? AN INVITATION AND A DIAGNOSTIC

So, you may have reached the end of the book, but it's the start of your 5D Service leadership journey. I wrote this book to make the case for why humans are valuable in service and offer a practical framework to leaders and influencers around the world. We must master the art of being human to ensure that humanity's destiny isn't automated away.

I hope I've clearly articulated an approach to reimagine the future of service in the world. I also hope that by this stage of the book, you've come to agree with two points:

1. *You believe in the value of human-to-human interactions in service.* If you're still a big fan of the idea that technology is the answer to all things service, and you're not entirely convinced that humans will bring value to service in the future, well . . . One of the wonderful things about humans is that we can simultaneously hold two seemingly contradictory views. You can believe that technology is shaping human existence and is the ultimate game-changer. At the same time, you can also believe that humans are the ultimate quantum computer, a part of mother nature and that we can outsmart any technology because we are the greatest technology.

To thrive in the digital era, you need both technology and human virtues to bring you excellent results in your relationships, projects and profits. The 5 dimensions are a way to ensure that we don't let our cleverness compromise our humanness!

2. *You agree that the future of service requires you, as a leader, to do things that are hard sometimes but not impossible.* Excellent service in any pocket of the world, in business or society, is not easy. It requires diligence, awareness and an intention to offer something great, something extraordinary. The 5 dimensions give you a way to embed practices and behaviours in your team environment that will make the hard feel more accessible and leading the herd less of an effort.

I and my team at ServiceQ feel a sense of urgency and insistence about 5D Service, which I'm sure has come across in this book. To help you get started on your 5D journey right away with no delay, I've put together a diagnostic for you, beginning on page 149, so you can assess where you're starting from and see, through the lens of the 5D Service framework, which areas need the most attention from you.

Why do you think humans serve best in the digital era?

The ultimate reward for writing a book of this nature is to have inspiring, courageous, bold and ambitious leaders like you becoming part of the conversation. I'm never too busy or distracted to read your personal notes or emails about this topic. To make this easy, my team at ServiceQ have set up a 5D Service page on LinkedIn at (www.linkedin.com/groups/12903445) that allows you and everyone else on this journey to share their stories.

Most of what needs to be done in the future of service is very humble, possibly invisible. No one may ever celebrate it. You might never get thanked in your lifetime. 5D Service may not win you fame or recognition – but future generations and emerging leaders will be grateful.

THE 5D SERVICE LEADERSHIP DIAGNOSTIC

This diagnostic will help you assess the current state of your 5D Service leadership. Go slow with it. Be compassionate to yourself, and treat this as an opportunity to see where the gaps are and what you need to hone in on as you begin your quest for 5D Service leadership.

How well do you, as a leader, create trust?

Dimension: Physical

Implementation: Create safety and support wellbeing

Aim: To maintain a healthy culture by focusing on physical and psychological safety as well as enabling a culture of wellbeing to exist among the work.

1. How often do you check in on your team members' emotional and mental wellbeing?
   ☐ Never ☐ Not often ☐ Sometimes ☐ Often ☐ Always

2. How comfortable do team members feel approaching you with concerns or issues?
   ☐ Never ☐ Not often ☐ Sometimes ☐ Often ☐ Always

3. How often do you and your team discuss and deconstruct failure/learnings?

   ☐ Never ☐ Not often ☐ Sometimes ☐ Often ☐ Always

4. To what extent do you prioritise work-life balance for yourself and your team?

   ☐ Never ☐ Not often ☐ Sometimes ☐ Often ☐ Always

5. How frequently do you provide resources or training on mental and emotional wellbeing?

   ☐ Never ☐ Not often ☐ Sometimes ☐ Often ☐ Always

6. In a journal or your own notes, recall and explain specific strategies you use to create a healthy culture of safety and wellbeing.

How well do you, as a leader, empower your team?

Dimension: Cognitive

Implementation: Empower decision-making and foster innovation

Aim: To empower teams to make better decisions and be more innovative in problem-solving in the moment.

1. How often do you delegate decision-making responsibilities to team members?

   ☐ Never ☐ Not often ☐ Sometimes ☐ Often ☐ Always

2. How open are you to receiving new ideas or suggestions from your team?

   ☐ Never ☐ Not often ☐ Sometimes ☐ Often ☐ Always

3. How frequently do you provide opportunities for team brainstorming and creative thinking?

☐ Never   ☐ Not often   ☐ Sometimes   ☐ Often   ☐ Always

4. To what extent do you offer autonomy versus giving directives?

☐ Never   ☐ Not often   ☐ Sometimes   ☐ Often   ☐ Always

5. How confident are you that your team can problem-solve and bend the rules to suit a situation in the moment?

☐ Never   ☐ Not often   ☐ Sometimes   ☐ Often   ☐ Always

6. In a journal or your own notes, write an example of a time you empowered a team member or fostered innovation.

7. When a crisis happens at work, how do you respond? List your approach, in order of thinking, in your journal.

How well do you, as a leader, motivate your team?

Dimension: Emotional

Implementation: Inspire emotional intelligence and praise to encourage behaviour

Aim: To motivate teams to apply the desired behaviours and self-regulate their emotional responses at work.

1. How well do you recognise and manage your own emotions in the workplace?

☐ Never   ☐ Not often   ☐ Sometimes   ☐ Often   ☐ Always

2. How often do you acknowledge and validate the emotions of team members?

☐ Never ☐ Not often ☐ Sometimes ☐ Often ☐ Always

3. How frequently do you praise team members for their achievements and efforts?

☐ Never ☐ Not often ☐ Sometimes ☐ Often ☐ Always

4. How regularly do you engage in self-reflection regarding your interactions with the team?

☐ Never ☐ Not often ☐ Sometimes ☐ Often ☐ Always

5. How well do you manage your emotions when under pressure?

☐ Never ☐ Not often ☐ Sometimes ☐ Often ☐ Always

6. In your leadership, what role does fear play? Are you using fear to motivate people? Write your answers in your journal or notes.

How well do you, as a leader, create a values-based culture for teams to connect to?

Dimension: Social

Implementation: Build teams and connections and align people with values

Aim: To inspire teams to connect and behave in ways that are aligned with the organisation's values.

1. How frequently do you engage in team-building exercises or initiatives?

   ☐ Never ☐ Not often ☐ Sometimes ☐ Often ☐ Always

2. How often do you emphasise and communicate the organisation's values to your team?

   ☐ Never ☐ Not often ☐ Sometimes ☐ Often ☐ Always

3. To what extent do you try to align team tasks and projects with organisational values?

   ☐ Never ☐ Not often ☐ Sometimes ☐ Often ☐ Always

4. How regularly do you encourage interpersonal connections among team members?

   ☐ Never ☐ Not often ☐ Sometimes ☐ Often ☐ Always

5. How often do you give the team a goal or desired state to strive for as a team, for the day or week?

   ☐ Never ☐ Not often ☐ Sometimes ☐ Often ☐ Always

6. If you were to create a trend line from a few years ago to now and a few years ahead, how are people relating to each other? Has trust increased or declined? Write your answers in your journal or notes.

   • Are people more willing to go the extra mile or not?
   • What's your evidence for any of these conclusions?

How well do you, as a leader, lead with a vision and create meaning at work?

Dimension: Spiritual

Implementation: Create vision and communicate purpose – evaluating the ability to lead with a vision and create meaning at work

Aim: To invite teams to see their work and efforts as a contribution to something far greater than their own self-interests.

1. How clearly have you communicated the team or organisational vision to members for that day or situation?
   ☐ Never ☐ Not often ☐ Sometimes ☐ Often ☐ Always

2. How often do you revisit and reinforce the vision and purpose with your team?
   ☐ Never ☐ Not often ☐ Sometimes ☐ Often ☐ Always

3. To what extent do you tie day-to-day tasks back to the broader vision and purpose?
   ☐ Never ☐ Not often ☐ Sometimes ☐ Often ☐ Always

4. How frequently do you seek feedback on your communication of the vision?
   ☐ Never ☐ Not often ☐ Sometimes ☐ Often ☐ Always

5. How often do you celebrate team and organisational wins, reflecting on the individual and collective contributions made?
   ☐ Never ☐ Not often ☐ Sometimes ☐ Often ☐ Always

6. In your notes, explain your specific strategies or methods to communicate vision and purpose.

7. What invitations to contribute have you extended to your team and why? How have people responded? Write your answers in your notes.

If you would like to discuss the results of the diagnostic above with one of the ServiceQ team or find out how we could partner with you to level-up the leadership and service in your organisation, head to our website **serviceq.co/contact-us** and let's do what humans do best: connect.

Let's connect

Jaquie Scammell is the founder of **ServiceQ**, a business that is passionate about reimagining everything service can be in the future. ServiceQ exists to provide learning programs and experiences to leaders and staff so they can elevate the standard of service leadership and customer service in their workplaces. Partnering with large organisations and notable brands across many different sectors, ServiceQ is honoured to share the inspiring testimonials from our clients, which outline the real and lasting change that our service transformation programs have made. To hear more about these go to **serviceq.co/testimonials**

To connect you with others on the **5D Service journey**, the team at ServiceQ has set up a website for latest activities and stories here: **5dservice.com.au**.

Join the 5D Service movement to view stories and contribute your own perspective to the 5D Service community.

Most of what needs to be done in the future of service is very humble. 5D service may not win you fame or recognition, but the emerging leaders and future generations will be thanking you.

NOTES AND FURTHER READING

Chapter 1: Customer service died in 2020

1. Centres for Disease Control and Prevention (CDC). (2021). *Youth Risk Behavior Survey Data Summary & Trends Report, 2011-2021*. www.cdc.gov/healthyyouth/data/yrbs/pdf/YRBS_Data-Summary-Trends_Report2023_508.pdf
2. Australian Bureau of Statistics (ABS). (2022). *Almost a third of employing businesses unable to find suitable staff*. www.abs.gov.au/media-centre/media-releases/almost-third-employing-businesses-unable-find-suitable-staff
3. 4 Day Week Global: www.4dayweek.com
4. ABS. (2022). *Business Conditions and Sentiments*. www.abs.gov.au/statistics/economy/business-indicators/business-conditions-and-sentiments/latest-release

Chapter 2: The future ≠ the past

1. Wardini, J. (2023). *101 Artificial Intelligence Statistics*. https://techjury.net/blog/ai-statistics
2. Bloomberg Originals. (2014). *Meet Amazon's New Robot Army Shipping Out Your Products*. YouTube; 4:50. www.youtube.com/watch?v=g6DIFpaoI6A
3. World Economic Forum (WEF). (2020). *The Future of Jobs Report 2020*. www.weforum.org/reports/the-future-of-jobs-report-2020
4. McKinsey & Company. (2017). *Jobs lost, jobs gained: Workforce transitions in a time of automation*. McKinsey Global Institute. www.mckinsey.com/~/media/BAB489A30B724BECB5DEDC41E9BB9FAC.ashx

5. Altman, S. (2023). *#367 – Sam Altman: OpenAI CEO on GPT-4, ChatGPT, and the Future of AI.* Lex Fridman (podcast). https://lexfridman.com/sam-altman

6. Artificial Intelligence Index. (2023). *Measuring trends in Artificial Intelligence.* Stanford University. https://aiindex.stanford.edu/report

7. Sinek, S. (2022) *Too many modern companies have replaced a person with a number and mistakenly called that number a customer.* X (Twitter) 12:15 AM; Sep 13. https://twitter.com/simonsinek/status/1569328978229428225?lang=en

Chapter 3: Why 5D Service is necessary for the digital era

1. Booth, E. (2022). Health staff cop abuse. *Herald Sun.* www.proquest.com/newspapers/health-staff-cop-abuse/docview/2756823541/se-2

2. Talkdesk. (2021). *The customer experience (CX) revolution in retail.* Talkdesk Retail Report. www.talkdesk.com/resources/infographics/the-customer-experience-cx-revolution-in-retail

3. Headspace. (2020). *Coping with COVID: the mental health impact on young people accessing headspace services.* COVID Client Impact Report. https://headspace.org.au/assets/Uploads/COVID-Client-Impact-Report-FINAL-11-8-20.pdf

4. ABS. (2023). *Consumer Price Index, Australia.* www.abs.gov.au/statistics/economy/price-indexes-and-inflation/consumer-price-index-australia/jun-quarter-2023

5. Employment Hero. (2022). *The Wellness At Work Report 2022.* https://employmenthero.com/resources/wellness-at-work-report

6. Ray, J. (2022). World Unhappier, More Stressed Out Than Ever. *Gallup.* https://news.gallup.com/poll/394025/world-unhappier-stressed-ever.aspx

7. The Business Research Company. (2023). *Antidepressants global market report 2023.* www.thebusinessresearchcompany.com/report/antidepressant-global-market-report

Chapter 4: 5D Service explained

1. Maslow, A.H. (1943). A Theory of Human Motivation. Washington, DC: American Psychological Association. *Psychological Review, 50* (4), 430-437.
2. CDC. (n.d). U.S. Department of Health & Human Services. www.cdc. gov/aging/disparities/social-determinants-alzheimers.html

Chapter 5: The physical dimension

1. Cuddy, A. (2015). *Presence: Unlock Your Inner Confidence to Embrace Life's Biggest Challenges.* United Kingdom: Orion Publishing Group, Limited.
2. De Mille, A. (1992). *Martha: The Life and Work of Martha Graham.* United States: Vintage Books.
3. Dhawan, E. (2023). *Digital Body Language: How to Build Trust and Connection, No Matter the Distance.* United States: St. Martin's Publishing Group.

Chapter 6: The cognitive dimension

1. McGilchrist, I. (2009). *The Master and His Emissary: The Divided Brain and the Making of the Western World.* United Kingdom: Yale University Press.
2. CBC. (2021). *Neuroscientist argues the left side of our brains have taken over our minds.* www.cbc.ca/radio/ideas/neuroscientist-argues-the-left-side-of-our-brains-have-taken-over-our-minds-1.6219688.
3. Hilton Segel, L. and Hatami, H. (2023). *Mind the Gap. McKinsey & Company.* www.mckinsey.com/~/media/mckinsey/email/genz/2023/04/2023-04-11b.html
4. Ferriss, T. (2016). *Tools of Titans: The Tactics, Routines, and Habits of Billionaires, Icons, and World-Class Performers.* United Kingdom: Ebury Publishing.
5. Chamorro-Premuzic, T. *Author Talks: In the 'age of AI,' what does it mean to be smart? McKinsey & Company.* www.mckinsey.com/featured-insights/mckinsey-on-books/author-talks-in-the-age-of-ai-what-does-it-mean-to-be-smart

Chapter 7: The emotional dimension
1. Fincher, D. (2010). *The Social Network* (Film). Columbia Pictures.
2. The Work of Edward Tufte. www.edwardtufte.com/tufte
3. Sivers, D. (2022). *How to Live: 27 Conflicting Answers and One Weird Conclusion*. United States: Hit Media.
4. David, S. (2016). *Emotional Agility: Get Unstuck, Embrace Change and Thrive in Work and Life*. United Kingdom: Penguin Books Limited.

Chapter 8: The social dimension
1. cdedman90. (2012). *Maumelle Wal-Mart Greeter Mr. Willie*. YouTube; 0:54 www.youtube.com/watch?v=qPMOYLA0KTo
2. Reed, J. (2023). *Chimp Empire* (TV miniseries). United Kingdom: KEO Films; Netflix.

Chapter 9: The spiritual dimension
1. Wheatley, M. J. (2017). *Who Do We Choose To Be? Facing Reality, Claiming Leadership, Restoring Sanity*. United States: Berrett-Koehler Publishers.
2. John Dewey views human beings as a highly developed state in the evolutionary process. We emerged through the progressively complex development of physical processes into organic and organic processes into mental ones. A human being is a complex whole of physical, organic and mental processes, with each higher process dependent on a lower one. The ability to develop meanings – rather than the existence of a special, separate consciousness or mind – characterises mental processes. For example, grasping meanings through language, which serves as a tentative guide to action, is a mental process. Likewise, the ability to envision and deliberate about possible future courses of action consists of working with meanings not immediately given in sense perception. Dewey rejects the notion that mind or consciousness is some separate entity existing above or apart from the natural world; rather, he regards the term 'mind' as a way of referring to those more complex processes of interaction of organism and

environment by which human beings create and develop meanings
as tools for action. https://sites.google.com/site/rythinkingtourspi5/
deweyandwilson

Chapter 10: Game-changers

1. Wheatley, M. J. (2017). *Who Do We Choose To Be? Facing Reality,
   Claiming Leadership, Restoring Sanity*. United States: Berrett-
   Koehler Publishers.

Chapter 11: The 5D Service leadership framework

1. Collins, D. https://dancollins.com.au
2. Edmondson, A. C. (2018). *The Fearless Organization: Creating
   Psychological Safety in the Workplace for Learning, Innovation, and
   Growth*. United Kingdom: Wiley.
3. Davis, T. (2019). What Is Well-Being? Definition, Types, and Well-
   Being Skills. *Psychology Today*. www.psychologytoday.com/au/blog/
   click-here-happiness/201901/what-is-well-being-definition-types-and-
   well-being-skills
4. Duke, A. (2018). *Thinking in Bets: Making Smarter Decisions When
   You Don't Have All the Facts*. United States: Penguin Publishing
   Group.